PLAY LIKE A

MAN,

WIN LIKE A

WOMAN

PLAY LIKE A MAN, WIN LIKE A WOMAN

What Men Know About Success That Women Need to Learn

BY

GAIL EVANS

BROADWAY BOOKS
NEW YORK

BROADWAY

A hardcover edition of this book was published in 2000 by Broadway Books.

PLAY LIKE A MAN, WIN LIKE A WOMAN. Copyright © 2000
by Gail Evans.

Broadway Books titles may be purchased for business or promotional use
or for special sales. For information, please write to:
Special Markets Department, Random House, Inc.,
1540 Broadway, New York, NY 10036.

BROADWAY BOOKS and its logo, a letter B bisected on the
diagonal, are trademarks of Broadway Books,
a division of Random House, Inc.

Visit our website at www.broadwaybooks.com

First trade paperback edition published 2001.

The Library of Congress has cataloged the hardcover edition as follows:
Evans, Gail, 1941–
Play like a man, win like a woman : what men know about
success that women need to learn by Gail Evans.—1st ed.
p. cm.
Includes index.
1. Businesswomen—Pyschology. I. Title.

HD6053 .E85 2000
650.1'082—dc21
99-462238

ISBN 0-7679-0463-X

20 19 18 17 16 15 14

For Julianna, Jason, and Jeffrey

CONTENTS

PLAY LIKE A

MAN,

WIN LIKE A

WOMAN

PREFACE

WHEN IT COMES TO ROLE MODELS, I WAS LUCKY. I grew up believing a woman could do anything—a conviction inherited from my mother. On the surface, my mother seemed like a conventional woman, a suburban housewife who tended to her home and husband's career. But all the while she was sending me the message that a woman is responsible for her own life, and that she should live it to the fullest.

My mother certainly did. Even while taking excellent care of her own family, she helped care for an "adopted" younger brother and sister from a local institution for juvenile delinquents, she taught at the Jewish Guild for the Blind, and as a volunteer Red Cross ambulance driver, she drove physically and mentally disabled veterans to picnics and ball games.

The manager of a chain of millinery stores in the 1920s, my mother gave up her career for marriage. But she never surrendered her drive or her belief in herself. Throughout my life, she gave me two sets of instructions: I must be a good and proper woman and I could be anyone I wished.

I took that advice to heart. After leaving college in 1963, I began a successful career in politics, working on Capitol Hill and at the White House. But when I married, like my mother and most women of the time, I abandoned my career for my husband's. We moved to Atlanta and then to the Soviet Union. After returning to Georgia, where I raised my three children, I began doing freelance research and public relations for international corporations. In 1980, I joined CNN, which was beginning operations.

Eventually I got the opportunity to create the first central booking department for a network (booking means finding the experts who appear on television). When CNN International was created, my responsibilities were extended to that network as well. In 1987, I was made a vice president; two years later I created *CNN&Co*, the first television talk show to feature women discussing the major issues of the day rather than simply "women's issues." After a promotion to senior vice president, I co-developed *TalkBackLive*, the first interactive television news program, and in 1996 I was instrumental in creating *Burden of Proof*, the first daily legal talk show on network television.

Along the way, like my mother, I have tried to give my time to others. In 1997, the same year I was made executive vice president of CNN, President Clinton appointed me to the Commission on White House Fellows. I'm a member of the Committee of 200, the International Women's Forum, the Citizens Review Panel of the Juvenile Court of Atlanta, and have taught a seminar on gender issues in business at Atlanta's Emory University Business School. And I serve on the board of several universities and not-for-profit organizations.

I also have a daughter and two daughters-in-law, as well as a granddaughter, all of whom I hope will feel as optimistic about being a woman as my mother and I have felt.

If they do, they are lucky. Over the last two decades I have met thousands of women who have told me they feel lost in a workplace where the men generally rule and the women generally follow. I have always tried to give these women my best advice, and I've always hoped that somewhere I would encounter a group that didn't need what I had to say.

Then I was invited to address the female students and alumnae at Harvard Business School. I thought here, if anywhere, is the place where women have conquered the workplace.

I was wrong. The Harvard women had learned their academic lessons well and risen to high positions, but they felt isolated. They still complained that they often felt lost in the male-oriented workplace, and weren't sure how to cope.

So I decided to write down the gist of all the talks my mother had given me, and all I have passed along to my own daughter and daughters-in-law, as well as all the hundreds of speeches I have made to groups of women around the country. Although television is the great medium of the day, I feel the best way to pass along history is through the printed word. Personally, I believe that I'm only as good as what I have taken away from the last book I've read.

What I want you to take away from this book is the ability to work in an office atmosphere where you don't say, "I didn't get what I deserved today because, as a woman, I didn't know how to play the game."

My greatest desire is that someday we will eliminate the conversation about inequality between women and men at work, so that when we come to the workplace as peers, how we do our jobs will be all that matters.

INTRODUCTION

Not long ago, I spoke at a small conference of successful businesswomen. Afterwards came the deluge, as one woman after another came up to me and asked for advice.

It always happens at these events. I speak, I listen, I hear the same words over and over—"baffled," "angry," "lost," "trapped," "stuck," "overwhelmed"— as each woman tells me she feels that she's gotten only so far in business and can't get any further.

One of the women at the conference told me she's a vice president at the Fortune 500 company where she's been working for two decades. In the last four years she has been given two new lofty-sounding titles, but no more power. She thinks she has hit a wall.

"Have you made it clear what you want?" I asked. "Have you taken any action?"

"No," she said.

Like so many women, she doesn't understand that when you have an ongoing serious complaint, you don't simply, meekly, live with it. You try to change it.

I told her that she needed to take action.

"What kind of action?" she asked.

"Anything," I said. "One action will lead to another. Talk to the CEO. Job hunt. Anything. Just do *something!*"

She sighed. "I don't understand. They know what a good job I am doing. Why don't they just reward me for it?"

With that attitude, she is losing the game.

If you don't read the directions manual when you start a game, you won't know how to proceed. You open the box, and in front of you are the board, markers, and dice, but you don't have a clue. If you're playing by yourself, you can improvise, but you may get it wrong. If you're playing with others, you can always follow their lead. But while they're focused on winning, you have to keep asking yourself if you're getting it right.

Whether that game is croquet, Monopoly, field hockey, or football, you have to understand the directions first. So why play the game of business any differently? Business is as much a game as any other board, individual, or team sports game. Consider all the metaphors like teamwork, making the right moves, playing your cards close to your chest, picking the best players for your team, rolling the dice, making a preemptive bid, raising the ante, finding the right captain, getting the team into position, hitting a home run.

The bottom line: When it comes to business, most women are at a disadvantage. We're forced to guess, to improvise, to bluff (which is not something we're always good at—see Chapter 5: Toot Your Own Horn). This is why so few of us play the game well, and even fewer find it fulfilling.

And what about men? They don't read directions manuals, you say. True. They don't need to. The male mind invented the concept of directions. It wasn't that they deliberately ignored women, or disliked what women had to say. Rather, as business culture developed, few women were around to help. Men wrote all the rules because they wrote alone.

Women have made great strides in the last century. But that progress hasn't always been smooth, nor has it been straight ahead. Sometimes it's even retrogressed. During the labor shortage in World War II, for example, women were called in to perform men's jobs, and they did well. But when the war was over, Rosie the Riveter was sent home, and women had to wait decades for another chance.

The best you can say is that we've seen a kind of creeping incrementalism. Large numbers of women dot the current workplace, but like trees on a mountain, you'll see fewer and fewer of them as you climb higher in the executive landscape, until you reach a kind of timber line where you'll find about as many women as you'll find magnolias.

Fortune magazine recently ran a cover story on the 50 most powerful women in America. Nothing wrong with that. What I found worrisome was that the positions these women occupied—group presidents, vice presidents, founders of their own businesses—were not comparable to what a similar group of men would have held. All the men would have been CEO of large companies.

Women now account for over 46 percent of the total U.S. labor force, up from 29.6 percent in 1950. But as of 1999, only 11.9 of the 11,681 corporate officers in America's top 500 companies were women. In 1998 it was 11.2. If this pace continues, the number of women on top corporate boards won't equal the number of men until the year 2064.

Last year only 3.3 percent of these companies' top earners were women, with 98 women holding positions of the highest rank in corporate America, versus 1,202 men. And 496 out of 500 Fortune companies had male CEOs. Many of America's favorite companies—General Electric, Exxon, Compaq—have no women officers at all.

And even when women do make it to the top, we don't make as much money: Compensation for the top-paid female officers ranges from $210,001 to $4.96 million, whereas men earn from $220,660 to $31.29 million. All in all, top female executives earn on average 68 cents for every dollar a male executive earns.

The reality in today's business landscape: A woman is most likely to occupy a position of power when she started, or inherited, her own business. We're not going through the ranks and making it to the boss's office, and that's where the power lies in corporate America.

What can—and should—a woman do? The answer would be easy if men and women were born with similar instincts and were similarly socialized. But that isn't the case. In fact, the general thinking among biogeneticists is that the social skills of males and females are inherently different. After that, according to the sociologists, they're raised in ways that accentuate that difference.

Let me tell you about my three children, two boys and a girl, whom I was committed to raising in a thoroughly nonsexist environment. Starting from day one, I could spot gender-based disparities among them. For instance, the way in which my sons and daughters nursed: My two boys behaved alike. They sucked until their stomachs were full, they burped, filled their diapers, and promptly went to sleep. It was a quick, effortless transaction. End of story.

My daughter gave a different performance. She sucked a little, she closed her eyes, then she'd touch, reach out, feel, suck, rest, try to open her eyes, burble, suck, touch, and so on. It was clear from the earliest moment that she was interested in some kind of social relationship with me. She wanted to know who I was and where she was. The boys just wanted to get their fill.

Nurture also has a say in gender distinctions. While teaching a course on gender issues in business at Emory University's Goizueta Business School, I asked my students about the games they played as children. What was the object of the game, how many other children participated, what lessons did they take away from them, and so on?

As usual, the sharpest young man was the first to raise his hand. "I always hung around with at least a half dozen other boys," he said. "We played games like pickup baseball, soccer, street hockey." He added, "The silliest question you asked was about the object of the game. We played to win. What else is there?"

"Oh, my God," interrupted a young woman. She explained how she usually played with one, or maybe two, other girls at a time, rather than a large group, and that they were always more concerned with building a friendship than with winning. Then she told us a story about playing a game of jacks with two friends at camp. When one of the girls was about to win, they all made up new rules so they wouldn't have to stop. "The object was to keep the game going as long as possible," she said. "And we wanted everyone to win."

The point is not that one of these perspectives is better than the other but that, from early childhood on, boys and girls play with different sets of rules. And because men created the rules in the game of business, and because women are only now trying to be effective competitors, we will prosper only when we are familiar with those rules.

None of this is to say that men are doing a bad, or a good, job. The business world is male-dominated. That is not a criticism nor a condemnation—it's a reality. Most of the time the male advantage isn't due to conscious discrimination against women. Like most people, men prefer to surround themselves with others who make them feel at ease. The relationship between men and women in business is not so different from that between a Caucasian Christian and an Indian Sikh, or an army general and a pacifist. Like attracts like. Differences create discomfort.

There is no denying that our society has created a division of labor between men and women, and historically one sex has tended to supervise certain tasks, and therefore write the rules. Recently, however, that division is becoming muddied, as both sexes are thinking about expanding the traditional boundaries, whether at work or at home.

For instance, some men are now staying home to raise children. The way we nurture our children in our culture is a female-determined system—these directions were written by women. It might turn out to be excellent for our children, however, if men have more of an impact on how kids are raised. We might have healthier children—just as we may have healthier corporations if women were to play a bigger role in them. The more heterogeneity there is at the table, the more likely we are to discover better solutions for everyone.

In the pages that follow you will find pointers to help you create your own personal directions manual for success. To become a player in the world of business, you have to know the prevailing rules that men play by—not because you must follow them word for word, but because you need to understand the playing field even if you eventually choose to make up your own game. It is not a level playing field if you don't know what to do on it.

1

THE OBJECT OF THE GAME

Action is the antidote to despair.
JOAN BAEZ, FOLK SINGER AND ACTIVIST

AS THE YOUNG MAN IN MY BUSINESS CLASS ASKED, isn't the object of the game to win?

But what is winning? Does it mean being the most powerful CEO? Does it mean being the one with the biggest bank account? Or is it the person who's the most feared?

For me, the object of the game is simply to feel great about what you do. That's the most important directive of all—because that's how you end up feeling fulfilled, and that's how you win.

I know for a fact that I have been successful because I've always loved my jobs. And believe me, these haven't all been well-paid positions in glamour industries—I've done everything from run the addressograph machine to fetch the coffee. But no matter what I've done, I've always been able to enjoy myself doing it.

For instance, when my kids were little, I took several years off to take care of them. To earn a little income along the way, I found a part-time job as a sales representative for a clothing company at Atlanta's semiannual merchandise mart. I then created a game out of it, seeing how much I could sell to stores even if they didn't need the line. I couldn't have done this forever, but while it lasted, it was fun. And I bought all my children's clothes (as well as mine) wholesale.

Similarly, not everything I've done on Capitol Hill or at CNN sounded exciting when it was originally proposed. But I've usually managed to make it so. For example, at one point my boss announced that I was going to revamp CNN's intern program. This came at a time when two of my children were already in college, and the last thing I wanted was to worry about other college-age kids. But I made the job challenging by taking on more responsibility than I had been offered, which turned out to involve recruitment and talent development. I gave my job so much visibility that when the new vice president of that area was announced, she was told to report to me.

So the ultimate winner in the game of business is not necessarily the person with the most power or the most money or the most fame. Rather, it's the person who loves his or her work. I know many miserable people with important titles. But I don't know anyone who loves her job who's miserable. It's that simple.

There's more: If you can love your business life, you'll be playing the game the way the guys do. They don't run out on the football field or stride into an important meeting wishing they were elsewhere. They are enthusiastic, eager to have an opportunity to satisfy their competitive urges.

Loving what you do is self-empowering. It makes you more brilliant, it gives you the ability to become a visionary, it helps you become the best businesswoman you can be. You improve your chances of rising to the top.

For some men, of course, loving the game is synonymous with material success. It's a basic cause-and-effect paradigm: If they get to the top and they get rich, they love it.

Women aren't as likely to love success as an isolated entity. We want to love our entire life. And that's fine. Unlike men, we don't tend to compartmentalize the various aspects of daily existence (see Chapter 5: Think Small). So it's hard to feel upbeat when we take a job that isn't intrinsically interesting—even if we see the possibility of success somewhere down the road.

Why do women have such a hard time understanding the importance of loving our work? My sense is that in our society, women are raised to feel comfortable in the role of nurturer, the ones who make things better for everyone else. We don't get permission along the way to love ourselves, or to love what we do, outside of our caretaker's role. Only in the last few decades have we learned that we can be the center of our own lives. And that means we, too, can start loving our jobs with the same enthusiasm as those guys who rush out onto the sports field and into the boardroom.

When you have a new baby, changing her diapers isn't drudgery, because it's not the diaper you're changing, it's the baby. You want to do everything you can for her. But when she's three years old, the focus shifts to the diaper, not the baby; so you toilet train her.

Likewise, in an office, you can teach yourself to do any job you're given and be okay with it. But ultimately, if you don't feel good about your job, you'll just be going through the motions, which means that you're turning off that button that I call possibility.

You can't play any game well if you don't enjoy playing it.

2

FOUR GROUND RULES

*I feel there is something unexplored about woman that
only a woman can explore.*
GEORGIA O'KEEFFE, ARTIST

A FEW YEARS AGO I ASKED THE STUDENTS IN MY
business course at Emory to interview successful
executives, both men and women. Their assignment
was to uncover the qualities of good leaders and
write up a report.

The assignment wasn't intended to be a gender
discussion by any means, but it was hard not to
notice that the words both the students and the executives used to describe men differed from the words
they applied to the women.

Some of the most common terms describing
male executives were: "quarterback," "absolute winner," "aggression," "boastfulness," "the desire to
win," "holding power," "tough-skinned," "having
fun," "part of a dog-eat-dog world."

These were the words and phrases used about women: "cooperation," "social involvement," "teamwork," "respect for others," "uncompetitive," "willing to share power," "concern for the harmony of the group," "feeling that everyone can be a winner," "wanting to be liked by all," "caretaker."

In the course of every discussion I've ever had about men and women, certain themes seem to appear; fair or unfair, professors, students, businessmen, and businesswomen all share the same vocabulary.

The same broad categories of women as "social" and "cooperative," men as "aggressive" and "tough" hold true in this book. Whereas not all men learned to play football or chess or poker, and not all women played with dolls or ignored competitive games, the majority of men and women were socially acculturated according to their sex.

Now, I know many men never played competitive sports or games while they were young. Certainly some women are stronger and more competitive than any number of men. And I'm not suggesting you should dismiss this book if you're a woman who is more comfortable with rugby than with dolls. I was a high school athlete, making all–Westchester County (New York) hockey goalie.

For the most part, however, the women's game was and is different from the men's. This is because men and women are wired differently, and we are brought up differently.

And when we are adults, we work differently. It is important for women to understand these differences, because the more aware we are of them, the more possible it is to gain access to power. Ignorance is never bliss. You cannot know too much.

Following are four fundamental ground rules underlying the strategies you need to understand if you are going to play.

1 | You Are Who You Say You Are

Playing any game means being faced with a variety of choices, and the game of business is no exception. You will do well only if you make your decisions from a position of power rather than a position of weakness.

Whenever I sit on panels I am always amazed at the wide variety of backgrounds among the women—they have seldom traveled the same straight and narrow path the men do. A woman's way has many more obstacles, mostly because we face this huge issue called family. I've never met a woman so alone that she didn't have an important personal relationship somewhere in her life, whether it's parents, sisters, brothers, or children. That means that many of us have gone back and forth between family obligations and careers, sometimes having to leave work, or change our hours, or take jobs in other cities.

Men generally don't feel that pull between staying home and advancing within the organization. So your career will be colored by a greater number of factors than his—your game board is more complicated.

Don't make your life more difficult by seeing yourself as a victim of this system. For instance, one of my closest friends has been with the same Boston-based conglomerate for 25 years. She's very successful, but she has reached the point where she's not going any further. She takes care of outreach seminars, she writes proposals, she organizes meetings, but the guys have taken her off the core line businesses. She complains that they don't appreciate her, that her boss is horrible, that her work is boring.

"Your kids are grown, you have money, your husband is prospering," I tell her. "If you're that miserable, get out."

She looks at me as if I've suggested she vacation on the moon. She accepted the role of being a victim years ago, and she's comfortable with it. In fact, she took on this role before anyone else in her company ascribed it to her, but now it's impossible for them to imagine her in any other way.

Too many of us tolerate the role of the passive, put-upon person, probably because it's the one most often taken by our primary role model—our mother. Remember when you used to get up late on a Saturday morning? Dad was calmly reading the paper, while Mom was complaining, "I've got tons to do so I'll drop you off at your ballet class on my way to grocery shop because your father's parents are spending the weekend with us and I don't have anything for dinner."

How many of us ever heard her say: "If you need to get to your class, tell your father. Also tell him what you want for dinner, and remind him to pick up his parents so they can spend the weekend. I'm meeting a friend for lunch."

Women have tended to live in the complaint, to grumble to our friends and our daughters about it—but until relatively recently, we haven't taken action to fix it. Like women who remain in unhappy or abusive marriages, we are often more comfortable remaining with the devil we know, no matter how unpleasant or disagreeable, than making a proactive (and therefore potentially risky) change.

As I see it, women have two options: to structure our world around our own choices, or to let someone else make the choices for us.

In the 1980 Olympics, the U.S. hockey team was expected to lose to the Soviet team. But no one told this to the U.S. players, who were clear they were the best team in the world. Eventually they said this to themselves enough times that other people began believing it too. By the night of the finals their conviction had become truth, and they won the gold medal.

If you want to take charge of your own business life, begin by sending out the equivalent message about yourself. Pick your goal and say it aloud to yourself. "I could manage this department. I would do an excellent job."

Picture yourself actually doing the job. What would it feel like? What does it look like? Try to make your positive fantasies real. The first step to being successful is convincing yourself that you are successful.

2|One Prize Doesn't Fit All

Have you heard the story about the couple who was seeing a marriage counselor to help save their disintegrating relationship? The husband says, "I don't understand—we have a great house, we have great kids, we have a great car—what do you want?" And the wife responds, "I just don't feel fulfilled." The man looks exasperated; he has no idea what she means.

Women demand a greater sense of fulfillment from our jobs than men do. The standard male-oriented rewards—money, power, prestige—

don't necessarily have the same sway with us.

Today women are learning to pay attention to our own needs, as well as everyone else's. This is helping us discover a new sense of freedom and independence in the workplace. Our jobs are not about our husbands or our children or our parents. Ideally, they are about us.

But can we handle this change? Many of us aren't always clear about what we want from this thing called a career. We anguish over whether it will be a career at all, or just a job to provide supplementary income. We obsess about whether it will have any real meaning to us, or whether we are doing it solely to please our family. We have incessant internal discussions over where we are going, and the route never seems to be as direct as we thought.

We live in what I call divine discontent. The work is never quite right, the company isn't either. Now, this feeling can keep smart women on their toes, because it can make them strive a little harder. But even so, such needless turmoil eventually wastes energy.

For most men, the actual job content isn't crucial. The trappings of success, such as title, prestige, and/or money can ameliorate the boring, unpleasant daily grind. Men reconcile doing work they don't like by getting high-profile rewards.

Consider the following: Over many years of public speaking I've often run into the CFO of a large manufacturing company who always tells the same story. Starting off in the accounting department, he slowly but surely worked his way up through one uninteresting position after another until finally, at the age of 60, he received his Glorious Reward and got the one job he'd always coveted. He is a smart and decent man. But every time I hear his speech, I shudder.

Unlike this male CFO, we women are much more likely to find an area in our company that we find fascinating and remain there for years. We tend to ignore the stars, bells, and brass rings that men consider necessary markers of success. For us, the ultimate reward can simply be the ability to say: "I feel great about what I'm doing."

Remember: Loving your job means you are the ultimate winner. But you must remain alert to all potential pitfalls along the way. No matter what the game, if two players are looking at a different goal, the manner in which they advance with the ball will differ.

Let's say you and John Doe start work the same day at the same level. John enters Sales, because he wants to be rich, and you enter Human Resources, because you're fascinated by interpersonal behavior. Fifteen years later, you look up to see that John is a vice president making $250,000 a year, and you're a vice president making $125,000. You think, "Did I do something wrong?"

No. And there's no reason to think you did—as long as you keep in mind that you and John Doe had different goals in mind. The rewards for being the vice president for human resources differ from those for being the vice president for strategic marketing. The title vice president doesn't have a salary attached to it. It depends on the perceived value of that job to the company.

When we choose to fulfill ourselves by what we do, rather than only what we make, we're not playing the game the way the guys are playing it. They are much more likely to be thinking about material success or power than fulfillment. Personally, I love the way women regard work, because our view is more holistic. But we must be aware that many times our decisions aren't going to be compatible with the male-dominated business culture, and if we go our own way, we may have consequences to pay.

If you opt not to play by men's rules, you have to be aware of the consequences. There are times when I've consciously decided to ignore the rules—but only when I was confident that I knew those rules inside and out, and understood that my male colleagues, finding my decision contrary, might lose faith in my ability to be a team player. You must be informed to take this path.

. . . . .

3 | Work Isn't a Sorority

A new CD-ROM game, Starfire Soccer, calls itself the first sports game designed strictly "with girls in mind." What does the manufacturer mean by that? It's a game where relationships are as much a part of the action as kicking the ball into the net. To quote the packaging material: "Winning isn't just about the final score. It's about friendship and fun too."

The boys' games, however, are about winning. The friendship part doesn't come into play—at least, not while they're playing. Relationships take place when the game ends.

Simply put: Women enter the job arena with a stronger urge to form and maintain relationships than men do. Whether we are talking to the dry cleaner, the cashier, or the boss, we want to know a life story, we want to exchange feelings, we want to turn the other person into just that, a person, rather than the other party in a business transaction.

Study after study has shown that women are more likely than men to make, and keep, close friends. In this new age of business, where maintaining and servicing clients is so important, a woman's disposition to form strong relationships will work very much to her advantage. A talent for working with people means you can make them feel comfortable and earn their trust, and that you're probably a good listener. It's amazing how often people will tell us exactly what we need to know, if only we can hear it above our own internal dialogues.

Women's relationship skills may be our secret to greater success. I know one woman who has risen to the top of her male-dominated advertising company not only because of her professional talent, but because whenever a relationship problem arises between client and agency (or more often, between the major players at her firm), she's the one each person confides in. In essence she has become the great conciliator when the major players aren't talking to one another. Her unusual combination of skills makes her an invaluable part of the company's operation.

There are hazards, however, to having a relationship orientation. For instance, women often interpret basic information in personal terms. Say the boss is talking with you in the hall and seems taken by your ideas for restructuring your department. Suddenly he excuses himself. You suspect he's changed his mind and doesn't like your ideas after all. Actually, he had to go to the bathroom.

I've watched women personalize the office to the point where they won't hire people they don't like—even if they are exactly right for the job. I've also seen women inflict a mortal wound on their own careers by refusing to cooperate with someone they have an aversion to. Your co-workers are not your friends or your family. You don't pick them and it doesn't matter whom you like or dislike. You simply have to work with them. Some of the most successful people I've known have refused to have any social contact at all with their co-workers.

The people you meet in business can be nice acquaintances, individuals you can have a good working relationship with, but the key word is "working."

Personalizing causes trouble. A guy running down the field with a football knows he has to make it to the goal line, and he'll run over anyone to get there. Just because the fullback is his friend doesn't mean he won't stick his cleats in the guy's leg—if he has to.

As little girls, too many of us were taught that in order to get what we want, we had to charm the other person, whether this was a friend, a teacher, or a parent. If you made Daddy feel good, he'd acquiesce to your wishes. But in the office, you usually receive a "yes" because your proposal has merit, not because you do. The guy who gives you the green light may not even know you. We don't always understand how someone with whom we don't have a personal relationship can respect us. I know many men in positions of power who dislike each other intensely, but when they're sitting around the conference table, you'd think they were joined at the hip. Their personal feelings don't matter. They don't want to be liked. They want to win.

To change the way you do business, where and how do you start? Train—as in any other game. It may fly in the face of everything that seems natural, but the more you practice *not* taking it personally, the more natural it becomes. In other words, you get there by doing it.

Women must understand that we're playing in a world where our opponents have been taught to hide their emotions. Joe Friday from television's *Dragnet* never said, "Just the facts, sir." It was always, "Just the facts, ma'am." If all the Joe Fridays want only facts from you, you'll irritate them if you give them feelings.

4 | You're Always a Mother, Daughter, Wife, or Mistress

I grew up with boys as friends, and so did my daughter. Society allows, and even smiles on, a young girl playing with a group of boys (if the boys will let her, that is).

For the most part, however, young males don't socialize enough with young females to accept them as close friends. And so it's rare, and seldom socially acceptable, to see a single boy playing with a group of girls.

When the time comes for that young boy who is now a man to mix with the opposite sex at the office, he is often at a loss. And when in doubt, he—like most people—stereotypes. Thus he tends to think of a woman co-worker as his mother, his daughter, his wife, or his mistress—even when she is very clearly none of the above.

Knowing this will help you understand male behavior patterns. If an older man has turned you into a Daughter, you can profit in innumerable ways—you'll be exposed to people and places that others won't see, and you'll be privy to conversations that will give you insight into how the business is run. Like any good father, Daddy will take care of you.

The downside? Men never think of their daughters as equals (much less their bosses). So after a few years of great opportunity, you become frustrated. And what do you do? You quit.

That's what I did when I was the Daughter, and it was one of the smartest moves of my career. I was sad to leave the job, but because it was clear I wasn't going to move up, I moved out—very, very carefully. Remember: It's important to maintain your father figure's support when leaving, because he can be a great help to you throughout your career, as mentor and counselor. Don't run away like a rebellious child.

Convince him he made it possible for you to move on, and ask for his support.

The Wife is the hardest role. Here you can be accepted on the job as an equal (more or less). But you're also encumbered with all the baggage a guy brings to the office from his real-life marriage: If he's married to a nagging woman, and you inadvertently start using language that reminds him of her, he'll probably respond by shutting you down the same way he shuts her down at home.

For example, my friend Julie once saw a male colleague march into the boss's office twelve times in one day to ask questions about a new project, and the boss didn't bat an eye. But just the second time she requested some information, he yelled, "Leave me alone. You're relentless."

When Julie heard her boss say that word, one he normally used to describe his wife, she suddenly understood his mind-set and didn't personalize the confrontation. She knew that, despite its downside, being a Wife has decided advantages. For example, the boss often cuts her off at meetings because he assumes he can tell what she's going to say. While this can be frustrating and even embarrassing, Julie knows that she'll have the opportunity to pass along whatever information she needs to convey at other times and places. In other words, she has the office equivalent of pillow talk—the boss speaks to her on his personal time.

Her co-workers only have the formal meetings to get their ideas across.

Basically, when you find yourself someone's Wife, you create ways to make it work to your advantage, unless it becomes thoroughly oppressive, and then you get a divorce.

Mother is a traditional role. She's the secretary who's been at the company 37 years, the woman who's been city editor for three decades, the executive who's had the same title since 1975. She's the one who welcomes the new people into the company, who makes sure the new vice president's kids have applied to the right school, who knows the office rules inside out. She probably invented half of them.

The bad part of being Mom is that mothers have covert power only. They get things done by innuendo and manipulation. The good part is: No boss can fire his mother. If you like the role, it's yours forever. Mothers languish safely until they retire.

As younger, more ambitious women have entered the workforce, the newer role for them is that of Mistress. Here you get to be a risk taker, you get to make decisions, you get to join the power structure. But you have to be very careful, because you're walking the tightrope of sexual tension. Very few of us know ourselves well enough not to get tripped up, and the consequences for your career may be especially severe if you're caught. You may lose your job as well as your reputation (see Chapter 6: They Can Have Sex. You Can't).

Tɪᴘ: When you're with your husband, get used to the idea that as far as his colleagues are concerned, no matter who you are, you are Mrs. Husband. Many years ago I accompanied my then husband to a Fortune 500 company's annual meeting, where he was giving a keynote speech.

The company's CEO had invited us to sit at his table with the company's other officers and their wives. After introducing myself, I told him what I did for a living, and the CEO asked me how many children I had. I brought up an important issue concerning his business, and he answered by telling me that his wife and I were wearing the same color dress. From then on I played the retiring wife.

As the evening progressed, the men began discussing a case of insider trading. Because of its privileged content, this matter should not have been discussed in front of an outsider, let alone a journalist. I excused myself from the table.

As I left, I handed the CEO my business card. I told him that although this evening I was simply an executive's wife, he needed to be more careful, for women are in the marketplace, too. (The next morning he sent me two dozen roses, thanked me for my discretion, and vowed never to make the mistake again.)

3

PREPARING TO PLAY

It had long since come to my attention that people of accomplishment rarely stay back and let things happen to them. They went out and happened to things.
ELINOR SMITH, AVIATOR AND WRITER

Learn the Playing Field

Suppose you're playing a game of chess. Would you use a backgammon board? No. But metaphorically, that's what many women do.

All games are played out on a structured field of action. If it's football, you're talking about a 100-yard-long field. If it's Chinese checkers, it's a board with a star pattern. Monopoly follows a one-way path along the perimeter of a square; a roller derby rink is round. Name the game—hopscotch, rugby, Scrabble—and you know the terrain.

The game of work is also played on a board or field, one that is traditionally shaped like a triangle or pyramid. At the bottom are the largest number of people; the farther up you go, the thinner the ranks, until you reach the very top, where there's only one person.

The advantage to a pyramidal structure is its clear line of authority, from bottom to top. Everyone knows who's calling the shots, and who isn't.

The downside is that it doesn't allow for much open and honest feedback. Compliance is rewarded over constructive criticism. Risk taking tends to be avoided. Yes-people tend to thrive.

The problem for most women is that we enter business with a different sense of the game board. We're more comfortable with the concept of a circle—the shape that represents the circle of friends we made as children. When we were playing house, we had long discussions with our friends about where to put each piece of furniture, which room to fill up first. We were all equal—in other words, there was no captain of the dollhouse.

Because everyone was free to talk with everyone else, the circle generated open communication. No one felt that she couldn't contribute or that her ideas wouldn't reach a sympathetic ear.

In the business world, however, the circle can be problematic. Too often the women who replicate these power and information circles are swamped with input. And because all this information can't be put to good use, unhappiness ensues. "The boss always claims that she wants to hear what I have to say," the standard complaint goes, "yet she never acts on it. Why does she bother to ask?"

But the primary issue for women isn't the advantages of a circle over a triangle, or vice versa. Just as when you play backgammon, you play on a backgammon board, if your company has a standard pyramidal structure, you play on a pyramid too.

Yes, we don't like to think of ourselves as mere pegs on some lifeless board. But men don't mind as much, and they don't mind marking you as a peg, either. They'll expect you to act like a peg, too. Labels bring clarity. If you're a vice president, act like a vice president, talk like a vice president, do the work of a vice president. There are no relationship issues here. It's a game board issue. You're sitting at a certain level in the pyramid. Respond accordingly.

For instance, a woman I know at one of the large consumer goods companies had an excellent idea for a new product and spent a great deal of time developing it with her closest colleagues. But the concept never flew. The reason? My friend didn't stop to think that at the top of her company was a small cadre of men who made all the final decisions.

Instead of seeking their support, she relied only on her relationship circle, not understanding that she had to enlist one of those men at the top of the pyramid to own her idea, so that when trouble happened, she was covered. Basically, her idea didn't reach fruition because she lost sight of the fact that a good idea isn't more powerful than the structure that must approve it.

I've always felt the best paradigm for the game of business would be a circle superimposed on a pyramid. This would allow interaction to take place among all levels of personnel, but would also provide a clear sense of hierarchy.

Finding a way to use our relationship orientation is one of the perspectives I hope women will bring to the game. In the meantime, if you're working in a standard hierarchical framework, you can only think circular if you've been given the freedom to do so from the people above you in the hierarchy.

Check Out the Team Culture

Up until a few months ago, Jane was a highly placed executive at a major media company. She had worked there for many years and was well regarded inside and outside the business. So when she quit to join the staff of a local not-for-profit organization, she surprised everyone—except those who knew her well, who were only surprised that it took her so long to leave.

Jane's issue: She held very strong political opinions, and her company's positions were generally antithetical to hers. Jane earned a good salary and wielded real power, but she always felt uncomfortable because she could never separate her inner beliefs from her company's outlook. Now she makes less money, but she's working for an organization she respects.

Many of us feel our company's values are as important as our jobs. Personally, I could not imagine working for a company I didn't believe in.

In the same way that men compartmentalize their work (see Chapter 5: Think Small), they compartmentalize their lives: This is my salary, this is my job, this is my family, this is my belief system.

Women care about the totality of the package. We want everything in our lives to feel right—not just the salary, or the power, or the prestige. If you are going to be successful, you must feel comfortable with the place you work. As you walk in the front door for the interview, recognize that you could be on the brink of your next relationship. You've had them with girlfriends, boyfriends, relatives, and so on. This company may be next.

Ask yourself questions about your potential employer: Does the company do something I can feel a connection with? Do I like its public image?

Does it stand for something I can stand for too?

Many years ago, when I was making $27,500 a year, I was offered a job as a producer on a Hollywood talk show. The salary: $125,000 a year—and this was just the first conversation. I could barely fathom what a grand sum that was. But the show was tacky, and the more I thought about it, the less the money impressed me.

I knew that if I didn't love my job, my performance would be second rate. So I turned the offer down. Not that I don't have plenty of bad moments at CNN, but at the end of the day, no matter what has happened, I'm genuinely proud of what I do and what my company stands for. I can say that to a large audience, or to myself, and know it's true.

The company's culture is more important than the position itself. You'll be happier with an average job at a place you love than with the ideal job at a place you loathe.

You'll also be happier in a place where you can feel comfortable. We tend to take on roles in our jobs just as we take on roles in relationships. Think about who you're going to be. The black sheep? The younger sister? The unattached aunt? The carefree daughter? The trustworthy confidante? Generally, your nonwork relationships dictate who you become at the office.

Unlike in your real family, however, here you have choices. Examine a new company carefully.

Ask yourself if it offers a relationship you'd enjoy. Are these people you'd like seeing day after day? Personally, I know if I went for an interview at an office where every woman was wearing a dark suit with a frilly white blouse and stiletto heels, I'd walk out the front door. That's not a uniform I feel comfortable around. Whatever makes these folks tick is only going to make me unhappy.

Likewise, I believe in an open-door policy at work, and I become angry when my colleagues shut their doors. To me, that's a management style that says, "We don't share." So if I walked down the hall and saw that everyone had shut themselves off, I'd walk out the exit.

Do you like your potential employer's office environment? Is it attractive? Could you feel comfortable there? Do people have private offices, or do they work in one great room? Is the building itself so unsightly you couldn't imagine walking into it five or more days a week? I know one major executive who turned down an important job because she couldn't face driving into the world's ugliest industrial compound every morning.

Even in these days of huge conglomerates, companies still have distinct personalities. If you work for General Electric, CEO Jack Welch and his values determine the corporate culture. At AT&T, Michael Armstrong does the same, as does Lou Gerstner at IBM. Oprah Winfrey does the same at Harpo Inc.; even small companies have personalities shaped by their CEOs.

Uncover that culture. Use your relationship skills. The person who interviews you probably has an assistant. Form a relationship with her. Since you'll probably be kept waiting for your interview, find out how the other women feel about the company, the job, the boss. Before a job applicant enters my office, my assistants always walk in the door with their thumbs up or down to let me know what they think.

The receptionist has a name. Use it. Take advantage of her attention. She'll probably offer you a beverage. Accept it. Most women don't, because they think the other woman will feel demeaned; most men do, because they know it's part of her job description, just as the water boy's job was exactly that—to get the water.

The receptionist brings you coffee, you thank her, and the opportunity for a relationship arises. I admit that it took me years to ask for that cup of coffee. Now, since I prefer tea, I do something else. When I'm offered coffee, I ask for hot water and tell the woman not to bother about the tea bags, because I carry them in my purse. That always makes for a conversation—most often she's a tea drinker too, or her mother is. Instant relationship!

Walk through the corridors. Do people look happy? Are they friendly? Do they seem your type?

Take a quick trip to the cafeteria or lounge, buy a cup of coffee, and listen. Are people complaining? Do they look miserable? Would you want to eat lunch with them?

Most of us put a great deal of time and attention into learning about the other important environments in our lives. If we're sending our child to school, we want to know everything about it—are the classrooms well-equipped, is there a good student-teacher ratio, does the school have a good reputation; we'll talk to a dozen other mothers. I know some women who'll spend months researching a possible vacation spot, and others who won't buy a house until they've practically camped out in it.

Your relationship with your workplace is one of the most important in your life. Make sure you do your homework.

Get Picked for the Team

A short time ago a friend was telling me a story about her son, who was trying out for his high school basketball team. Because he's considerably shorter than his classmates, he arranged a basket shooting display for his coach to show that his skill compensated for his size. He had practiced on the garage hoop several hours a day for the better part of two years. The strategy worked. He landed a spot as a guard.

When he announced the good news to his family at the dinner table that night, his father was delighted. But his sister, looking at him with the disdain that only a younger sister can muster, said, "I'd never want to join any team that didn't already want me."

Carry this kind of experience over to the job interview. The typical guy, who knows what it's like to sit on the bench waiting to play, arrives prepared to sell himself. His every movement says, "Come on, coach, let me in the game."

Most women, on the other hand, spend a lifetime hoping to get noticed. We're taught that it's more polite to wait to be asked—to go out on a date, to get called on in class. (Not surprisingly, studies show that girls are twice as likely to raise their hands in class if boys aren't around.) We don't grow up learning how to sell ourselves the way men do.

But on a job interview, you have to sell. And you have to sell with whatever you've got. Even if it's your first job and all you can say for yourself is that you're a well-organized, hardworking person, then do it. Let them see how accurate you are.

You're going to be bumping into male-female stereotypes all the way, so be alert. The first one to consider takes place before the interview starts: punctuality. Yes, men are as tardy as we are. But the cliché of the man who's late isn't so much a part of our culture as the constantly late woman, who's so overwhelmed with her life that she can't manage her time.

Don't expect to get away with a lie. I don't believe people who excuse their tardiness by saying they were in an accident. Why are they sitting in front of me without a smudge or a worry on their face? Shouldn't they be at the hospital or the police station?

The Problem: When women act in a manner that confirms stereotypes, we get slammed. It's even worse when those stereotypes hit a nerve. For example, if your interviewer has a perpetually tardy wife, and you show up ten minutes late, he will be angrier at you than at an equally late male applicant.

Good Strategy: Do some reconnaissance. Go to the interview site the day before so you don't get lost. Is the site near routine traffic jams? Is there a lengthy security check? What about parking—is it convenient and plentiful?

Other stereotypes walk right into the room with you. Boy's games teach them to develop their physical power; girls' games don't. Thus men are more apt to comfortably stride into the room, sit down, and look large.

I'm not saying you should strut into the interview like a football player, but you don't want to appear meek either. Find a way to exude self-assurance and physical presence. Every move you make matters. If your handshake is a wet dishrag, for example, you make a statement. I noticed the importance of this the other day when a newscaster came in for an interview as an anchor. When she put out her hand to say hello, her grip was solid. I was immediately more available to talk to her; I knew that a whole person was present. Too many women don't grip the other person's hand when they shake it—in part because we are not comfortable showing physical strength, but I'm also convinced that our experience taking a man's hand is colored by our dating years. Holding hands with our boyfriends was usually a passive, even a submissive, moment.

Do you make eye contact when you meet someone? Since women are taught to be modest, we seldom penetrate with our eyes. Furthermore, because we're trained in intuition and relationships, we often avoid looking directly into another person's face, because it may seem rude.

Or perhaps we're afraid of seeing truth. Look into a man's eyes and you'll know if he loves you, said our mothers. Many women have told me that they avoid eye contact with interviewers because they're afraid they'll see the job isn't theirs.

Bear in mind: Some interviews will be great and some will be terrible. That's a fact of business life, and there's no reason to believe you did something wrong. If the exchange was indeed that gruesome, the company may well be the wrong place for you.

That man eyeballing you is looking for someone who can make a difference to the team, someone who has the skills to compensate for the team's current weaknesses. When you exude comfort and confidence in the interview situation, you're letting him know you can do what needs to get done.

Basically, business is one long interview, so you might as well learn to do it well now.

GAME HINT: Women often think we must be smarter than men to land the job, but you can outwit yourself by being too smart. If you come to an interview armed with a dozen Serious Points you want to make, you may become so concerned with showing off your knowledge that you don't hear the actual conversation.

Wear the Right Uniform

Men have it easy when it comes to dressing for success. Basically, they have a uniform—the suit. This means that when they introduce themselves to a prospective boss, he's not paying attention to their outfit. He's focusing on their personality, their handshake, their resume. (We always joke with the male CNN anchors that the only item of clothing they can change is their tie.)

A woman's wardrobe, however, is a vital part of our presentation. It tells our colleagues what we're all about. Do you want others to think you're a plodder or an iconoclast? Are you creative, gregarious, secure? Are you conservative, timid, self-conscious? Your wardrobe has the power to convey all these messages, and as you move up the ladder into management it will prove either an asset or a detriment.

The primary message your clothes convey: I am suited up. I am ready to play. I am wearing the appropriate uniform to achieve my goal.

Once you're on the team, find your personal comfort level. I wore dresses for years, but now I prefer pants suits, which allow me to take off my jacket during the day. But even on casual days I keep a blazer handy so that I'll always look appropriate for an important impromptu meeting. I particularly like blazers with oversized pockets, where I can stuff my wallet and ID card if I don't want to carry my handbag. In the context of business, a purse can be a distraction.

The history of our wardrobe often reflects the history of our careers. One very smart woman I know can never really get ahead. Overweight, she dresses like a hippie in shapeless clothes designed to hide her body. Her company has carefully moved her out of positions of power and excluded her from meetings with outside executives. The more distance between her and the big bosses, the more she hides in her clothing. Her fears, first reflected in her dress, have become a self-fulfilling prophecy.

A sales executive I know at a California financial company earns a good deal of money, but she's not as high up in the company as she'd like. The reason: Her outfits are attractive but a little too tight. They show off her excellent figure, but they are inappropriate—so much so that her male associates feel uncomfortable around her. One colleague told me he was reluctant to have business dinners with her alone because he worried about what his wife would think.

A woman can also use her wardrobe as strategy. One high-priced lawyer tells me that the more difficult the negotiation, the more feminine she dresses, because she wants the opposition to forget how tough she is. On a normal day at the office, however, she wears a basic pants suit, to show her partners that she is as much of a power player as the rest of them.

The higher you progress up the ladder, the more apt you are to establish your own personal style. Secretary of State Madeleine Albright always wears a large pin on her lapel. It's the most noticeable aspect of her wardrobe, and its purpose is to suggest her individual style and her femininity without deviating too much from the appropriate uniform of the highest ranking member of the president's cabinet.

The bottom line: Dress for the team, but do it with confidence, creativity, and within the range of your own personal comfort. Clothing telegraphs to the world not just who you think you are, but who you want to be.

GAME HINT 1: Like it or not, our clothes frequently reflect our mood. Many of us have fat clothes, depressed clothes, angry clothes. When I'm at my heaviest, I wear unattractive outfits. It's a mistake. When a woman's outfit looks only half-pulled together, people tend to think her life is equally disorganized.

GAME HINT 2: One of the major rules in dressing for television is to avoid anything distracting—jangling bracelets, dangling earrings. This is true for business too. Such accessories are only appropriate when you want to distract—and in my entire career I don't recall ever wanting to do that. You could chair the most important meeting of your life, be at your most brilliant, look your very best, but if you're wearing elaborate jewelry, that will be the first thing people notice, and perhaps the last they remember.

Set the Right Goal

Not long ago, after giving a speech on the West Coast, a member of the audience approached me and told me about her seven-year plan. She was only a manager now, she explained, but in three years she was going to be a vice president, and four years after that, a senior vice president. She concluded by asking me about my own plans for the future.

I told her that to the best of my knowledge, I was going to be eating dinner shortly. I wasn't being flip. I've just never had three-, five-, ten-, or any other year plans. I've always felt that if I can tell what's going to happen to me in the next few days, life is good.

A plan can provide a sense of security. It gives you a tangible goal, something you can write down on a piece of paper and reassure yourself against. "Two years from now I will have a Big Title and make $75,000. Four years from now I want a Major Title and $150,000. In seven years, I want the Ultimate Title, I want my salary to double, and I want a big bonus too."

But rigid goals and five-year plans remind me of one of the most serious flaws in the old communist systems, one which helped assure their downfall: Inflexible goals impede new possibilities. No career is completely linear—it jigs and jags and crosses and turns. The mark of a good player is the ability to improvise; sticking to a specific plan leading to a specific goal limits your ability to do so. The woman who has that great new job you didn't even apply for probably never made a plan. While you were busy figuring out your own Step Seven, she was taking advantage of a challenging but unconventional spontaneous opportunity.

A great career is seldom reached by a ladder of small steps. If all you do is move up little by little, the ladder will go on forever. You don't get where you want to go incrementally. In most companies, the person recognized as a star is either the one who has made the great move or the one who has outfought the opposition. Stars don't wait for the future. They make the future happen.

Combine good strategic plays with vision. Goals stop possibility; vision creates them. Have a basic sense of what you want and where you want to go, and then try to visualize yourself there. Guys do that. From the moment they walk into the building, they see themselves in the CEO's suit. Every guy in my office feels he's a potential CNN president. Few of the women do— we rarely see ourselves higher than the highest-ranking woman we know, and she's seldom a CEO.

Having a vision also means taking advantage of any opportunity that can make it real—from moving into a fading department with turnaround potential to jumping on a promising new project that everyone else fears.

And be sure that your vision keeps pace with current reality. Jan Leschly, CEO of the drug conglomerate SmithKline Beecham, tells a story about his goal as a young tennis star to play center court at Wimbledon. He practiced and practiced to achieve this end, and one day he did indeed play Rod Laver at center court. As Leschly says, everyone has heard of Laver, but no one has heard of him—because he lost. His vision wasn't to win at center court. It was just to play there. Having vision isn't enough—you have to keep adjusting it to ensure you don't limit your options.

Personally, my professional goal was to feel good about my work, to grow, and to be appropriately compensated for my contribution. As for doing well, I just assumed I would succeed. I've never wanted to do nonsuccessful. I learned long ago that if the quarterback hands you the ball, you don't wonder if you're going to make the touchdown. You assume you will.

Instead of spending your day saying, "Why?," learn to spend it saying, "Why not?"

4

HOW TO KEEP SCORE

There is no point at which you can say, "Well, I'm success-ful now. I might as well take a nap."

CARRIE FISHER, ACTRESS AND WRITER

HERE'S JANIS, WHO'S BEEN A VICE PRESIDENT AT a large company for several years. She is a strong supporter of women in her industry, and her division has more women working in it than any other in her company.

It is also one of the most successful, but you wouldn't know this from walking around her department. The women who work for Janis don't have the same large offices and the same impressive secondary staffs as the men in similar positions elsewhere in the company.

Janis's bosses are not slighting her. She never asked for these things, because she didn't think they mattered. Janis didn't demand a huge office, because she was more comfortable with a smaller room, which fit her self-image. She didn't notice that outsiders who walked through her corridors thought the guy in the large space next door was more important than she was. He wasn't, but how would anyone know that?

To a guy, everything counts. The size of his office, the size of his staff, the size of his salary, the size of anything that can be measured. And they're always keeping score. Watch guys on the tennis court. Unlike women, who often suggest we "just volley for a while," the men want to start a game right away. After all, the object is to win. You can't win if you don't know who's ahead.

Perks are like your wardrobe; they introduce you to your business associates. And they either speak of power or they don't.

When we've done a good job, we can feel satisfied if the boss praises our work and gives us a dutiful raise. But if we don't have the sense to ask for staff, stock options, benefits, cars, club memberships, severance packages, guaranteed performance reviews, we probably won't get them.

Several years ago, following a promotion, a male colleague wondered if I'd been given the allowance for a big car or a small car. I didn't let him know that I wasn't aware of any car allowance. When I checked into the matter, I was horrified to learn that everyone else on my level had been offered car money long ago. Once I bothered to find out about it, I was smart enough to demand the large car allowance. The company agreed to my request without hesitation.

I've often noticed that there are some fairly young guys in the company whose jobs aren't clear to me, but when you walk into their well-appointed offices, you can't help but be impressed. Sometimes it's because the young man knows how to play the game and has asked for fancy surroundings. Other times it's because he has a mentor who wants him to look hot. A skillful mentor will make sure that the junior people on his team look powerful, because that's how he looks powerful too.

Recently a male executive was given a raise and promised a new office near mine. His boss decided the new room wasn't large enough, so he had the walls torn down between two smaller offices to create more space.

These tearers-down-of-walls are seldom women, because to many of us, such ostentatious land grabs feel greedy. Worse, we often receive validation from other women when we don't try to rack up the points. There you are, sitting around the coffee lounge with your friends, telling them how you and three guys were offered new offices, and one of them wasn't nearly as nice as the others. The guys were relentless in their pursuit of the three nice rooms, while you finally said, "This is ridiculous.

I'll take the small office. I can put nice pictures in it and make it look fine." The other women agree with you.

I can't imagine a woman saying to her crowd, "I stood there and screamed and stood my ground until I wore them all down and got what should have been mine in the first place!" If she had, her friends would have thought, "She must be out of her mind."

There is a lot of support from our female business associates for doing the right thing, particularly when the men are doing something wrong. But is this support always helpful?

The guys are always figuring out who's ahead and who's behind, and we're not. That means, while they're racking up points, we can be perceived as losers. We're thinking, "I'm doing a good job so I don't need these symbols of success," while he's thinking, "Man, she sure doesn't know the score."

GAME HINT: Say you're sitting around in the lunchroom with a cup of coffee and you have a sudden inspiration about your new project. You mention it to a few people at the table. You take little heed, but the guy sitting across from you is taking notes.

Then, at the next concept meeting, you hear him presenting your material as his. A foul play? Not really. At work, you can't look at a referee and yell, "Time out!" There is no time out. Everything you say and everything you do is part of the game. It's only practice when you're not keeping score— and the guys always are.

KEEPING SCORE WITH DECOR: I know a woman whose brains and zeal have helped her achieve success in the corporate world, but you wouldn't know it by looking at her office. Because she knows her present furnishings are perfectly functional, when the bosses offer her a new chrome desk, a black leather chair, a fancy credenza, she declines. And since she dislikes working in a space that isn't familiar, when they suggest it's time to paint or recarpet, she politely says no, even though the other executives on her level all have freshly painted corner offices with large windows.

This is how she manages her own home: She buys lovely furniture at the thrift shop and repaints or restains it herself. She also excels at keeping her household within her budget.

Not surprisingly, her climb to the top is faltering. Whenever she has meetings with other executives or outside vendors, she has to use someone else's office, because it's more comfortable, and that means she's never seen in the power position of sitting behind her own desk, running the meeting. People have begun to think of my friend as an oddity, a pack rat who toils away in a cramped space with dumpy furniture.

If pressed, she would probably tell you that her superiors must be grateful to her for saving the company so much money. (It is true her frugality has saved money, but only a negligible amount—a tenth of a percent of her department's total budget.)

As for myself, I have always made the mistake of using recycled furniture, because it seemed silly to buy anything new when the company storehouse is filled with excellent used chairs and desks. I think of myself as a good girl who doesn't waste money, but I doubt anyone else in the company knows—or cares—about my thriftiness. It took writing this book to make me realize I need to upgrade my office.

5

PLAYING THE GAME: FOURTEEN BASIC RULES FOR SUCCESS

A woman is like a tea bag. You never know how strong she is until she gets into hot water.
ELEANOR ROOSEVELT, FORMER FIRST LADY AND SOCIAL REFORMER

MANY YEARS AGO, AS MY BIRTHDAY WAS APPROACH-ing, I began fantasizing about the wonderful presents my husband might give me. Feeling particularly romantic that cold winter, I remember dreaming about bouquets of fresh-cut flowers, particularly my favorite—roses.

When the day arrived, my present turned out to be a television set with a pair of headphones, which meant that I could tune in my favorite programs while my husband watched his sports events.

In all fairness, he had spent time and money on his gift, and he genuinely expected me to like it.

Anyway, I had never actually told him I wanted something romantic, like flowers.

That's the key fact. I never told him. My thought was, "If he really cares about me, he'll know what I want. If I have to tell him what I want, I don't want it."

Every time, at every seminar and speech I give, when women hear that story, they nod. We all seem to recognize that sentiment.

Now translate that sentiment into business.

Say your immediate goal is the Paris assignment. Your boss has been talking about opening up an office in France for a year now. It's your dream. If you're not paying attention to strategy, you'll strategize like this: You'll obliquely mention how much you enjoy European travel. You'll say how you've signed up for French lessons. You'll talk about your growing interest in French cuisine.

But as you do all this—and as you continue to perform better than anyone else in your department—some guy down the hall will march into your boss's office and convince him he's the best guy for Paris.

And your boss will give him the assignment.

When you protest, the boss can honestly answer, "I didn't know you wanted it."

"Didn't you get my hints?" is a poor response.

Games teach guys to go after what they want.

No matter what they're playing, they learn that you don't win if you don't identity your goal and strive to achieve it.

So what should you do to get the Paris job?

You don't have to do it a man's way. But you do have to:

1–Understand the difference between how he plays the game and how you play it.
2–Recognize that for the time being, his way of playing is the accepted way.
3–Decide if you want to change the way you play.

Following are 14 rules that will instruct you to play the game a man's way—and win. Each direction includes a scenario, the typical moves men and women make in it, and some thoughts to consider.

1 | Make a Request

SITUATION: The Paris post is available (see above).
HIS MOVE: He asks.
HER MOVE: She hints.

To put it bluntly, asking is the only way to get what you want.

Obvious? Yet I can't tell you how often I've heard stories of women who have entered contract negotiations hoping for a large raise and were offered a small one. They felt disappointed, they felt cheated, they wondered if they had done something wrong. But did they object? They did not. Instead, they told the boss, "Thank you." But they certainly complained in private.

It's not an accident that the infamous line from the movie *Jerry Maguire*, "Show me the money," was spoken by a man.

Afterwards, the boss may appreciate how courteous the woman was, how easy it was to do business with her, what a pleasant time they both had. But the boss gave the big raise to the guy who came in and demanded it.

Over the years I have seen many women succeed and many women fail. The reasons they succeed are numerous, but the reasons they fail fall into a few identifiable categories, and near the top of that list is the inability to understand the meaning of the word *no*.

Women have been acculturated to believe that *no* means NO!, and so we often won't make a request if we think we're going to get a negative answer. To a man, however, *no* suggests a range of possibilities: *No, maybe,* or *later*.

Men learn at a young age that *no* is a relative rather than an absolute term—a temporary rebuff rather than an outright rejection. The boy knows the original *no* wasn't necessarily an outright rejection. It doesn't mean you can't go out and play some other time. It just means that right now, at this moment, you can't play.

Likewise, if he's made the team, but the coach won't let him in the game, he'll approach him again later, when someone gets injured or fouls up. "Hey coach," he says, over and over. "I can do it! Give me a chance!"

Even when men suspect that they're going to get an unfavorable answer, they still charge ahead and ask the question. So they get a *no*. They shrug it off, take it back to their office, struggle with it, then they come up with a plan to change the negative into a positive. They think, "It wasn't the right moment to ask, I didn't ask the right way, or use the right words."

A person's reaction to the word stems from the power of the word itself. Do you take *no* as a personal rejection, or do you take it as a piece of new information that you must work with?

Because we personalize situations, we hear *no* as a comment on our abilities, a sign the relationship between us and our superiors has failed. The result? We stop trying. The female definition of the word *no: Absolutely not, how could you even ask?*

THE PROBLEM: Because you're afraid of being rejected, you never ask for what you want.

WHAT TO DO: Imagine the worst that can happen if someone tells you, "No." It's not a tragedy. It's not a fatal injury, only a setback.

So I say, speak. Say it aloud in your office. Nothing becomes real until you say it aloud. Women lean toward internalizing and anguishing. Yes, if you don't ask for what you want, you won't end up being embarrassed. Yes, if you keep your desires hidden, you'll feel safe. Yes, you can't fail if you never tell anyone what you want. But at the same time, you can't succeed.

So look at the wall and announce, "I want to be vice president for strategic marketing." Say it to the window, the ceiling, the desk.

Now sit back and decide whether this is really what you want. Either you'll think, "Yes, I'll make a great vice president." Or, "No way. That's a job I would hate."

I firmly believe that we live into who we say we are. The first step to becoming a general manager is to begin thinking of yourself as a general manager, and to begin saying it aloud, over and over. Keep repeating it until you're so comfortable with the idea that eventually, it becomes who you are.

2 | Speak Out

SITUATION: A meeting with the boss and a dozen staff members.

HIS MOVE: He's not completely up to date on all the information, but he talks knowledgeably at the table whenever he has a point.

HER MOVE: Only 95 percent confident of her stuff, but better prepared than anyone else in the room, she has a nagging doubt that keeps her from speaking up.

As I said earlier, men are comfortable holding forth. From the time they are young their opinions are solicited, they're pressed to speak up. They are rewarded for the right answer, and a wrong answer bags them a hearty congratulations for trying.

Take this model to the office: We've all noticed that men can feel confident expressing some of the most ridiculous ideas imaginable, spouting notions and hatching plans that make us cringe. They know that the only ideas they'll be remembered for are the good ones. The other 95 percent may amount to a hill of beans, but those few good ones make them king of the hill.

Men talk a lot. Women don't talk enough—even seasoned executives. Consider this: Because I run the CNN editorial board meetings, I determine which two dozen of my associates to invite to the informal lunch with our guest speakers, who range from world figures such as Mikhail Gorbachev to writers like Maya Angelou. Over the years, the women seldom spoke up in the question-and-answer sessions. And if one did, and a man started talking at the same time, she would instantaneously shut down. Eventually I established private ground rules for the women: If you don't ask a question, you don't get invited back to the next meeting.

Now they talk, because they have to. And they ask superb questions.

Related to the issue: Boys grow up playing so many games and sports that they learn how to lose. They grasp that setbacks are temporary, that anyone can make a comeback, that saying the wrong thing in a meeting is not the end of the world.

Women feel like failures when we make a mistake or lose face. Because achievement is our trump card, we think we shouldn't say a word unless we're 100 percent certain of what we're talking about.

THE PROBLEM: If you don't talk, no one will know you're there.

WHAT TO DO: Study your surroundings and act accordingly. For example, if you're in a meeting, observe how the others act and interact. Do they laugh, tell jokes, and eat? Are they serious or relaxed? Do others defer to the big cheese, or does each of them act like big cheeses? Do they speak

up, or does the boss do all the talking? Every meeting has a different culture. It's your responsibility
to figure it out.

3 | S p e a k   U p

SITUATION: The boss has ten minutes in which
to hear two short presentations.

HIS MOVE: He gives his report loudly and
clearly in less than five minutes.

HER MOVE: In a barely audible voice, she talks
for almost a quarter of an hour.

When a guy is playing a competitive game,
there's little time for chatter. Say he's on the basketball court with five seconds left to play and his
team, behind by one point, has the ball. When
the coach calls him over, he doesn't ask questions
about the history of the game or his feelings
about last year's coach. He says what he must as
forcefully as the situation warrants, and only
that.

Men will tell you that women are too timid
when they talk at the office, or too evasive, or too
circuitous, or too unsure of themselves.

There's a female executive at a Fortune 500
company whose male peers have nicknamed the
Let-Me-Ask-You-a-Question Lady. She has plenty
of smart questions to ask, but she doesn't seem

able to get them out without first asking, "Let me ask you a question . . ."

It's the worst strategy in the playbook. You never ask if you can ask. You just ask.

Because we were taught to speak our mind only reluctantly, our vocabularies are saturated with such phrases as "I don't mean to interrupt you, but . . ." Or "I know that you're very busy, but . . ." Or "Everyone may have thought of this idea before, but . . ." Or all those other phrases that end with a *but*. Why do we need to apologize for what we're about to say? Why can't we just say what we need to say, and say it quickly? When you ask for permission to speak, you're putting conditionality instead of strength around a statement. Conditional talk doesn't have much power.

Even if you can get past the apologies and the circumlocutions, there's still the issue of volume. Women often talk so softly in business meetings that few people in the room can hear us well.

To some degree this can be seen as another form of learned behavior—a result of not having been encouraged to speak as forcefully as men. When we have to quiet down our kids, however, we never seem to lack the ability to turn up the volume.

But speaking forcefully isn't really about speaking loudly or softly. It's about learning how to use your voice effectively. Even if you have a small voice you can sound powerful—as long as you believe you have a right to speak.

Careers don't progress if no one can hear the point you are making, or if half an hour after you whisper your brilliant idea, someone else restates it more powerfully and gets the credit. It's not really your idea unless you're willing to stand up for it and give it power. You don't score a goal if nobody knows you did.

THE PROBLEM: Your speaking manner is weak.

WHAT TO DO: You must speak in a convincing and unconditional manner. That doesn't mean you have to talk like a man. It doesn't have to be, "I'm going to kick your butt if you don't do what I ask." But you need to practice how to talk in a way that gives you power.

If you have to, go home and talk to a blank wall. Say, "I've had enough." "I don't want to do this today." "I won't be cut off in the meetings anymore." Speak loudly enough so that if there were someone in the room, no matter where he or she was, you could be heard.

Throughout corporate America, women speak from the place called no-permission. We speak softly, we speak timidly, without authority or power. Not long ago I was on a panel with two knowledgeable women who lost their chances to shine because their voices were too tentative. Everyone else in the room stopped listening to them, while the one man who talked gave a forceful presentation. And in the end, he was the person who was asked all the follow-up questions, even though the women were really the experts. Later the women complained to me that it was just another meeting dominated by men. But I told them they were as much to blame.

All women should take at least one course in presentation skills. We have no hesitation about signing up for a tennis lesson to learn how to perfect our backhand, yet we seem unwilling to do the work to speak authoritatively. Learn to project your voice. Do you honestly think that Peter Jennings and Tom Brokaw were born speaking like anchormen?

Have someone videotape you as you speak, and then watch the replay. This is tough, I know. There's a reason I stay on this side of the camera. But I have forced myself to do this dozens of times because I always learn something.

Obviously, you can't change your voice completely, but with training, most voices can become more powerful, more effective in business situations. Your voice is an instrument, like a piano or a violin. To succeed, you must play it like a master.

4 | Toot Your Own Horn

SITUATION: The big boss is making his monthly tour through the corridors.

HIS MOVE: He walks out of his office, introduces himself, and mentions his newest project.

HER MOVE: Confident that the boss knows who she is because her work has been excellent, she stays inside her office, assuming that performance is all that matters.

When I was growing up, most of my friends lived in nice houses and had affluent parents with nice cars. We knew few people outside our close circle, but every now and then we'd play with another girl who lived in the next town over. She seemed just like us, but one day, when we finally visited her, we discovered that her house was bigger than all of ours, her yard was twice as large, her parents had three cars. Slowly it dawned on us that her family was very, very rich.

She clearly had taken pains to hide it, because she didn't want to show off. After all, we were being raised to believe in equality, and that meant that we didn't bring attention to ourselves. If one of us distinguished herself in some way—if we won a prize at school or got a new dress—our friends were supposed to say how wonderful we were, how pretty we looked. We were allowed to fish for these compliments, but we couldn't solicit them directly.

Boys' games teach them to stand out any way they can, to step boldly out of the box. How else will the coach notice them? You don't get into the game by mumbling to the coach that the guys already on the field are a lot more capable than you are. Boys exaggerate, they boast, they brag.

It's the same with business. Part of getting ahead is getting noticed. And the woman who gets noticed is the one who makes sure that her bosses know how good her work is.

Taking credit for your accomplishments is part and parcel of your job performance. Yes, the company hired you to keep the accounts in order. But they also hired you to join the ongoing conversation, which means that whenever they discuss new projects or look for solutions to old problems, they want your input. And how will your bosses know you have good ideas if no one has told them how talented you are?

THE PROBLEM: You're uncomfortable in the spotlight. You feel your work should stand for itself.

WHAT TO DO: Make sure everyone notices what you do. Stick out your hand and introduce yourself. Let people know that you're smart, that you've met your numbers, that you're on top of your operations.

But you can't do this the way a man does. He can get away with boasting. You can't. When guys brag, it reminds them of being on a team. When women brag, men and women hear rudeness and pushiness.

You must learn to be your own public relations person in a way that's comfortable for you and works within the culture of your office. So we have to find ways to toot our own horns without making ourselves or our associates uncomfortable. For most of us, the best personal public relations is accomplished in a relationship context. Rather than stand up at a meeting and talk about yourself, find a more personal way to get the word out.

TIP 1: Update your boss on your progress; write him a memo every couple of weeks to remind him subtly that you're an important member of the project. Don't be grandiose. Be clever—hide your self-promotion in your description of what your team is doing. Let everyone's good work reflect on you. And when there's a victory to report, make sure you're the first one to announce the good news. If he's astute, he'll realize that you were a key player but he'll appreciate your team move.

TIP 2: When a new boss walks the corridor, introduce yourself. But don't stop there. Introduce yourself to everyone: people in the elevator, people walking down the hall, people in the parking lot. And don't worry if that stranger turns out to be a junior employee, because you never can tell whom she knows, or who she will be in the future, or when she might give you that little leg up.

TIP 3: When you attend an office party, don't socialize only with your friends. A casual introduction can lead to something big. Say a manager has been assigned to a new project and has been told to hire one of three people. He doesn't know any of you, but his assistant says, "I met Jackie at the Christmas party, she's really smart." Or he thinks to himself, "Didn't I talk to a Jackie at the company picnic? She sounded very capable."

Women are champions of small talk. So talk small. When you meet someone at the company picnic, if you don't know the right opening line, tell him his daughter ran a great race, or that his son plays baseball like a pro. If you're thinking, "That's not how I want to be known," I say, "Why not be known that way—at first?" Men love to hear nice things about their families. You're not lying. You're starting a relationship.

Use your intuition. Size up what works with the person you are talking to. If you don't think he wants to talk about his kids, try something else: his summer vacation plans, his professional training, or his new car.

TIP 4: Most large companies have newsletters. If yours does, volunteer to write for it. And don't be coy if someone wants to cover your department. Give the reporter leads. Introduce her to your staff. Everyone in the company reads the newsletter, and everyone will learn more about what you do.

· · · · ·

GAME HINT: Closely related to boasting is bluffing, a concept that has loaded connotations for women. Aren't we raised to be virtuous, truthful, full of integrity? I can barely think of any woman who pretends to know more than she does. If anything, we veer in the other direction. Because we want to be absolutely sure we know what we're doing, we prefer overpreparation to bluff.

Males learn to bluff in every childhood game they play. But there is no bluffing in dolls or playing house, because these games aren't about winning and losing. You only need to bluff when you want to win.

Like it or not, part of being good at a job is making it up as you go along. There will always be times when you won't know it all. And you're not going to convince anyone that you're confident if you look terrified—which is why a poker face is one of an executive's best friends.

5 | Don't Expect to Make Friends

SITUATION: A new colleague moves into the next office. Although pleasant and cooperative, she makes it clear she's not interested in making friends.

HIS MOVE: He doesn't care.

HER MOVE: She feels hurt. She feels guilty. Did she do something to offend her?

. . . . .

Aware that schools all over the country are now encouraging women to play sports, I was curious to talk to a young friend who plays varsity soccer at a small East Coast college. She's a good athlete and her team does well. But last week, after watching her first soccer match between two top NCAA female teams, she was in shock. "They were so mean," she said. "They play for keeps. We like to win, too. But mostly we want to have a great time with each other."

Things are changing—very slowly. While at some colleges, in some athletic programs, some women are learning to play to win, that is not the prevailing attitude. The emphasis on victory is still a male concept. Playing to make friends is not. When was the last time you heard a bunch of guys, back from a serious football game, whooping it up and saying, "What a wonderful weekend, we met some really nice guys on the other team. Too bad we lost"?

Work is no more about friendship than a tough competitive sport is. Men are clear that business is business, and personal is personal. When they disagree over job-related matters, they don't see each other as being unsupportive or uncaring or disloyal. They know that they can have a tough fight on Friday, and still drink a few friendly beers together on Saturday.

For many women, our relationship with a co-worker is so significant that we forget the importance of appropriate distance.

For instance, the bookers at CNN are responsible for finding the right expert to feature on air. The job of the researchers is to do the prescreening, which involves talking to the chosen guest and going over his or her material. Sometimes, after that preinterview, a researcher decides a booker has selected the wrong person, and she says so. I can't tell you the number of times that tempers have flared and friendships have ended over these disagreements. The booker takes it personally that her close friend the researcher has undercut her.

I tell the booker and the researcher (when they're ready to listen) that our work is not about friendship. It's about getting the job done in a professional way.

The ideal work situation for most of us is to run the ball toward the goal line, then pass it to our best friend who lobs it to our sister who throws it over to our cousin and then back to us to score. But what happens if your best friend or sister or cousin doesn't like the play? Are you going to stop the game while you're in danger of being tackled by your opponents and accuse her of disloyalty?

THE PROBLEM: If you insist on being close friends with co-workers, you may soon have a lot of ex-friends—and an ex-job.

WHAT TO DO: Keep in mind that your job is only

a part of who you are. Your work is your work, and your life is your life. Decisions and comments that make sense for work may not make sense in any other context. Always remember that making friends is not an objective of a business situation. It's a by-product.

GAME HINT: One of the major myths in the business world, and one primarily perpetuated by men, is that women don't support each other. Not so. Women do a great deal to help each other. And don't forget it.

If there is any truth to the myth at all, it may reflect the way the male hierarchy often pits one woman against another as the designated female for the job, creating an unpleasant competition.

But more often this myth stems from overpersonalization of work-related issues. And when the resulting disputes become public, it's usually the men who disseminate the story to all.

Years ago, one of my peers, Joanna, confided to a male co-worker, Jordan, that the only other woman at her level had promised to support her at a meeting, but had backed down when confronted by the chairman. Joanna expressed her surprise and anger that her friend hadn't stood by her, but her friend later explained her reasons, and Joanna accepted her apology—and that was the end of it, she thought.

But Jordan never let the matter drop. To this

day, whenever the two of them are in a meeting and the conversation turns to an issue concerning women, Jordan will look at Joanna, wink, and say, "You, of all people, know exactly what I'm talking about. Don't you?"

No matter that Joanna has told him repeatedly that her friend had explained her silence. Jordan refuses to drop the subject because he wants to believe their enmity persists. He also enjoys sharing it with other men—which he does, inside and outside the office.

So even if you can't help but become angry with a female co-worker, for the sake of the rest of us, keep it to yourself.

GAME HINT: You can't expect to make friends of everyone. And you can't make everyone happy.

Another friend recently approached me about her husband, who was having trouble with his boss, a man I've known for years. "My husband is so smart," she said. "You know that. Maybe you can help."

I told her firmly that it would be a grave mistake for me to get involved (and that what she was proposing was a possible first step to divorce court). The instinct to help out any way you can is the sign of a good heart, but it doesn't make for good game strategy—and it's certainly not the way guys play the game. Can you imagine a man making an appointment to see his wife's boss to help her advance up the corporate ladder?

I don't care who you are. You can't please everyone. If you try, you'll end up taking care of not only your kids, your spouse, and your parents, but also your assistant, your boss, your vendors, your accountants, and God knows how many others. First and foremost, your job is to do your own job.

6 | Accept Uncertainty

SITUATION: The boss gives everyone at a certain level new areas of responsibility.

HIS MOVE: He doesn't tell anyone he's uncertain how to proceed, and he forges ahead.

HER MOVE: She is so worried about her new responsibilities that she finds it almost impossible to get any work done at all.

Fact: Unlike men, who owe their success to a variety of factors, women assume we get ahead because we're better at our job than anyone else. I don't think any woman ever believes she was promoted for any other reason than her excellent performance.

As a result, over the years we've adopted a perfectionist model. We don't say we know something unless we're completely confident we do.

Men are brought up to feel comfortable with a

generalized sense of the right answer. If they're familiar with the game board, they believe they can smell out the correct way to proceed.

If I wasn't aware of this fact already, teaching at business school gave me proof positive. Whenever I asked a broad question about a subject, the guys nodded their heads knowingly. They guessed I wasn't going to quiz them. Who knows, maybe if they racked their brains, they really could come up with an appropriate response if called on.

The women, on the other hand, always waited until they fully grasped the particular point I was making. They weren't about to nod their heads unless they felt they could make a solid contribution to the subject.

Think of the way men play games. They don't run out on the field, saying, "Who the hell knows if we can beat these guys!" They're filled with bravado, bluff, swagger. They psych themselves up. They say, "We can do anything!"

Whether they can or not, they know that if they start the game feeling confident, they have a much better chance of triumphing.

THE PROBLEM: If you have to feel completely safe before you move on or up, you'll never move at all.

WHAT TO DO: Have faith in your general ability

to perform, and stop worrying about whether or not you have the specific competence to do a new job. You'll figure it out soon enough. There's no such thing as Completely Certain—not in business, not in life. Part of being good at a job is learning how to make it up as you go.

That's not being a liar. That's being able to improvise. Most difficult situations that arise at work have no precedent. A great executive can always figure out how to do that which hasn't been done before.

7 | Take a Risk

SITUATION: You feel stalled at work, and the boss tells you that the only way to get ahead is to break out of the box and take the occasional risk.

HIS MOVE: He takes the risk.

HER MOVE: She becomes so preoccupied with weighing the pros and cons that she never takes any action at all.

How do you break the training of a lifetime? From the get go, men are encouraged to take chances. We are told not to. Little boys are told to get out there and fight. We are told not to. He's 4'2", and he's happy to be guarding a boy who's 5'8". He learns what risk is.

Women are brought up to be physically careful,

to avoid situations that are potentially dangerous. Don't jump off that wall. Don't touch that dog. Don't play near the water. The last thing our parents want is for us to hurt ourselves. What if we scarred ourselves for life? What man would want to marry us then?

But you can't get ahead without making risky moves. No one who is content to play safe ever sees her career skyrocket. No one who's afraid to stretch the boundaries ever becomes CEO. Being passive gets you nowhere.

Risk seems frightening, because it involves being active. What if I make that move and get fired? What if I accept that new project and make a mess? Why take a chance at all? Why rock the boat?

Fact: All boats rock. If you're going to be successful, you're going to make mistakes, and at some point you're probably going to get fired. But not to worry: Mistakes and firings can mean that you've done something out of the ordinary or that someone has noticed you. In fact, as long as mistakes represent the exception and not the rule, they are often signs of success. A career made up of many pluses and a few minuses is the career of a winner. "I don't care if a manager makes five serious mistakes. At least that person is making decisions and learning from them," says Microsoft CEO Bill Gates.

Even more difficult for many women to accept: The things we think of as risks are often not risks at all. Let's say you've been working at the same job for seven years. You're bored and you can't figure out exactly where you're going next. The guy sitting across from you is in the same position, but he's thinking that it's time to move on. One day he walks into the boss's office, announces he has a new job, and quits.

You may think he's making a mistake by leaving his secure, if unexciting, sinecure. Actually, while you've been obsessing about how bored you are, he was doing his job, plus all the work that goes with finding a new position—putting out feelers, sending out resumes, talking to head-hunters, and so on. He's not randomly rolling the dice, he's got them all loaded. And while you're still trying to justify staying put, he's in a new world, with more money, better contacts, and new status.

THE PROBLEM: You can't get ahead because you're terrified to take a risk.

WHAT TO DO: People who take risks are people who have their fear under control. Without fear, it's not a risk.

Take small risks to prove to yourself that you can manage your fear. Set up minor tasks that you can afford to fumble. For example: Say a competent woman arrives at her office an hour before—and leaves an hour later—than everyone else. She doesn't get much done in those hours; she's just proving how hardworking and dedicated she is. She's confusing *busy* with *productive*.

For this woman, real risk would be to come in at nine and leave at six. I've recommended this schedule change to several women, and all of them were able to face their fear that they owed their success to their long working hours. After shortening their day, they discovered no one else thought less of them for spending fewer hours in the office—and they still got all their work done.

Start a conversation with someone you're afraid of, or someone you suspect is twice as smart as you are, or someone who's obnoxious. Or, walk into the office of someone you think is mad at you. It helps you define your own boundaries when you can sense that another person's bad mood has nothing to do with you. Try thinking, "He must have had a fight with his wife last night." Very often, when someone's yelling at you, he's probably just angry. The "at you" part only means that physically you're in close proximity.

If risk continues to scare you, consider that you're taking risks every day. Driving to work is a risk. Eating raw fish is a risk. Life is filled with risks, but you've become so inured to most of them you don't notice.

There really isn't a fundamental difference in how men and women approach their personal fears. It's just that men are more used to confronting them than you are. He's taking his 236th risk, you're taking your fifth. Of course you're more scared.

In the modern business world there is no such thing as safety, which means that risk is a relative term. Something is risky only if you don't know what you are doing. Otherwise, you're simply calculating the chances that a potential move will be good or bad, and then taking action. Fear is part of the braid of success—don't let it paralyze you.

Yes, you can fail, but if you're ready for the possibility, you have a backup plan. Today's failures can pave the way for tomorrow's successes.

8 | Be an Imposter

SITUATION: A man and a woman have been promoted to positions of power.

HIS MOVE: He arrives at his office, admires his fancy desk and furniture, and contemplates his new responsibilities. He realizes that there's much he doesn't know about his new job, but he tells himself that if he's gotten this far, he'll probably go further.

HER MOVE: She arrives in her office, sees the fancy furniture and the corner view, and feels uncomfortable. She knows she worked hard to get here and that no one deserves a promotion more. "But now I'm in over my head," she thinks. "It's only a matter of time before they figure out I'm an imposter."

The one game that most girls learned to play well was The Game of Knowledge. This is the one we learned in school, the one where we were rewarded (with good grades, parental approval, teacher attention) for being a good student, for doing our homework, for being prepared when called upon.

Since we're only now learning about the game of business, we still rely on the Game of Knowledge. As a result, we usually enter the workplace convinced that the only way to advance is to master our subject backwards and forwards. We collect information, we accumulate anecdotes, we do whatever it takes to get the job done.

When we're ready to make a presentation, we make sure we haven't missed a single fact, and we enter the conference room trailing highlighters, annual reports, and computer printouts, thoroughly overprepared and overeducated.

Feeling that you know everything about your subject means you don't have to worry about being caught off guard. But it has a downside: No one knows everything. Eventually a colleague will ask you a question that you can't answer. And when that time comes, you suspect that you're an imposter.

This is the horrible, sinking feeling, experienced by the intelligent and the hardworking, that success is accidental. This imposter syndrome causes us to live in constant fear that we will be discovered, that our inadequacies will be exposed, and that we will be humiliated, demoted, dismissed.

Women who suffer from the imposter syndrome frequently expend as much energy trying to figure out how to survive their presumed unmasking as they expend doing the actual job.

They also become very good at convincing themselves not to take risks, because moving into any new territory makes them even more vulnerable to exposure.

The real truth is, we *are* imposters. Each and every one of us, men and women alike. None of us has a grasp on all the facts. Think about it. Does any one of us truly know everything there is to know about raising kids? No. But that doesn't stop us from doing it, or from doing it very well.

Business is no different from life. Men know that. They fake it whenever and wherever they have to. They go from one place to the next, gathering as much information as they can, and the closer they move to the top, the more they rely on improvisation, self-confidence, and the generalized ability to draw on past experience rather than book knowledge.

In business, when you're doing something new, there is no safety net. That is nerve-racking. That is also how creative business ideas are advanced.

THE PROBLEM: With every new promotion and every new step comes the feeling that you're an imposter waiting to be exposed.

WHAT TO DO: Accept the fact that there isn't one of us who can honestly say that he or she knows everything there is to know about the job, or who can't be caught off guard, or who couldn't be replaced one day by someone more talented. And believe me, the same is true of all of your bosses.

More important is how you talk to yourself. Do you tell yourself you are an overachiever who has no idea what she is talking about? Or can you admit, "I'm in new territory, but I wouldn't be here if I weren't competent and knowledgeable. So instead of focusing on what I don't know, I'll focus on my store of information and learn the rest as I go along."

Ask yourself reasonable questions. What are the things that someone in this job should know? Do you know them? If not, how long would it take you to learn them? Did your predecessor know more at this stage than you do?"

When I was first asked to start a central booking department for CNN 17 years ago, I had no idea what form it should take or what help I needed to set it up. But I did understand that the company's president had selected me for two reasons. First: He had confidence in me. So instead of worrying that he'd chosen the wrong person, I looked on my job as an adventure and decided that the worst outcome would be to return to my old job—which I'd always liked anyway. Second: The president knew I wouldn't besiege him with questions. I'd just do the job.

Bosses delegate work to you because they want *you* to figure it out. If they'd wanted to figure it out themselves, you'd be superfluous.

Replace your imposter scenario with a self-confident one. Confidence is half of the game. Whenever you can convince yourself you'll score, your chances improve. When you convince yourself you'll fail, your chances diminish. I know that whenever I think I'm going to drop the ball, I frequently do.

9 | Think Small

SITUATION: The company is in crisis mode and everyone has been given more responsibility.

HIS MOVE: He assumes he can do what has to be done, and slowly and methodically gets to work.

HER MOVE: Feeling overwhelmed, she frets away valuable time.

Boys like games that are straightforward. They want to get from point A to point B, and they want to win while doing it.

Girls prefer games that offer a variety of possibilities. In the dollhouse, for example, there are dozens of options to consider—where should the living-room furniture go, where should Daddy sit, would Baby be happy with a view of the backyard?—and a multitude of tasks. Rather than racing to reach some kind of goal or endpoint, girls enjoy drawing out the game, making up stories about the occupants of each room, inventing relationships, personal histories.

By and large, as these games turn more complicated, as the relationships between the characters grow more involving, the more interested a girl becomes.

These games teach us to become multitaskers, and this ability to multitask becomes part of a woman's existence. As in the dollhouse, there are myriad responsibilities to attend to in a real house every day.

Unfortunately, women are apt to bring our dollhouse/real house sensibility to the office. As a result, not only do we have to focus on our new important project, we also worry if our mother went to her doctor's appointment; if our daughter did her home-work; if our son got beat up by the school bully; if the cleaning woman changed the beds in the guest room, which makes us remember that we still haven't bought groceries for our sister's visit this weekend, or that we need to get the slipcovers replaced.

At home, overwhelmed or not, we cope with our responsibilities because the solutions are well-defined. We can deal with a crying baby by picking her up and soothing her. Unfortunately, we can't do the same with the budget projections. Spread sheets don't calm down with a hug and a burp.

"It's too much," we say. "I can't get it done." "I'm giving up."

A recent international poll conducted by the Roper Organization shows that not only are female executives more likely to say they are "super-stressed" than men, but that white-collar and blue-collar women are equally likely to feel this way.

THE PROBLEM: You feel so overwhelmed by the amount of work on your desk that you can't concen-trate.

WHAT TO DO: I remember the exact anecdote that helped me figure out how to cope when I felt over-whelmed. It concerns the 1950s English track star Sir Roger Bannister, who, along with his competitors, was trying to run the first four-minute mile.

Bannister's coach knew Bannister could run a quarter mile in one minute, sometimes even a little less. So he devised a clever psychological trick: He taught Bannister to stop focusing on the event as one mile long and instead to think of it as four quarter-mile sprints, and to run each one in a minute or less.

Bannister was able to reframe the picture and he broke the record—and was knighted for it two decades later.

By making the ultimate goal seem impossible to attain, we can become immobilized, unable to understand how to get from here to there. But there are few projects that can't be broken into smaller, more manageable pieces, making the distance between here and there seem a great deal closer.

The guy down the hall is clear about this. He knows the drill. He takes the first thing he has to do, concentrates on it, finishes it, then moves on to the second thing, concentrates on it, gets it done, and so on down the line.

Men can work like this because the larger picture doesn't distract them. As we have seen, men compartmentalize. Their lives have parameters; they walk into the office, and they're clear—this is my office, this is what I get paid to do. Like racehorses, men don't mind wearing blinders to help them focus on what needs to be done.

We would have a fit if anyone put blinders on

us, because blinders would mean that we couldn't communicate with the other horses, or see which horse is walking down the lane, or who's being fed what. But blinders can be useful. They lead you where you want to go—the finish line.

A woman's work is never done, goes the old saying. Don't you believe it. You can always get your work done, when you focus on the pieces one by one.

10 | Don't Anguish

SITUATION: Two days are left before the big presentation and the work isn't finished.

HIS MOVE: He doesn't let on that he's worried.

HER MOVE: She tells her friends that she knows she won't be ready.

I once knew an exceptionally talented woman who worked for a large company, where she was known as the local Ally McBeal. She told her troubles to everyone who would listen. Every mistake, real or imagined, became the subject of a long conversation. Every self-destructive thought was verbalized. Every dreary moment was grist for the rumor mill.

The woman saw nothing wrong with her behavior. She even volunteered that her therapist (whom everyone heard plenty about) recommended that she share her feelings as often as possible.

As was frequently pointed out, her therapist didn't have to share an office with her. Those who did found themselves so burdened by her inappropriate disclosures that they turned her into a pariah. No one would volunteer to start a project with her. No one would want to take a trip with her. Her career slumped, which made her worry more, which made her talk more.

Remember this: Guys wear their game face. Even when the odds are against them, they still try to look as if they're going to win. And who knows, maybe they will.

Girls are brought up to be nice. In turn, we want everybody and everything else to be nice too. When they aren't, we anguish openly about anything and everything—what's the best restaurant for a client luncheon? Are these the right clothes for the meeting? Is promotion really a possibility? Are the budget projections accurate? Is the weather good?

I'm not saying that guys don't worry. Of course they do. But they know that when the competition is intense, you don't let your anxiety show—unless you have a compelling reason to do so. Say the substitute comes into the game to help charge everyone up. He doesn't tell his teammates that he should be looking after his grandmother, and his foot hurts, and he doesn't want to have to compete against his cousin on the other team.

Women are more apt to show vulnerability than guys in all areas of life; we were encouraged as young girls to tell Mommy what's wrong. We got attention for sharing our problems. "Does it hurt? Mommy will make it better," were among the kindest words we heard.

Today you're not worrying about your skinned knee but about tomorrow's presentation, and you're tempted to share your fears with your colleagues. What you want is the same kind of reassurance you got when you were young. "You'll be fine, you'll do great."

But the guy in the cubicle next door isn't Daddy. He has no interest in your inner turmoil. And you don't want him to know. Because if he does, someday he could use it against you. That may be unfair, but that's business.

THE PROBLEM: Nervous and stressed out, you want to discuss your problems with others.

WHAT TO DO: Don't. Anguish in private.

But if you absolutely feel you have to confide in a co-worker, pick someone you can trust, someone who won't use your anxiety against you, someone who can help you focus on what needs to be done, rather than on what went wrong.

Bear in mind: If you're anguishing all the time, you must ask yourself if your work is really the source of your difficulties—or could the real problem be a personal issue that you're reluctant to discuss with your family or close friends?

HINT: If you're a boss, part of your job is to maintain control. That doesn't mean that you can't show you have questions or problems. If your department isn't going to meet its numbers, for instance, it's your responsibility to put your group on notice. But if you start telling everyone that the project is doomed to fail, either you will undermine everyone's self-confidence and the project truly will collapse, or your employees will think of you as a worrywart and they'll stop listening to you.

11 | Follow the Team Leader

SITUATION: Eight people are working on one project under one team leader.

HIS MOVE: He contributes as best he can and reports regularly to the leader.

HER MOVE: She voices her doubts about the project long after it's begun and subtly tries to do things her own way.

Jill, after starting as an assistant, worked her tail off at her company until she was made a vice president. Last fall she was one of many people attending an industry convention. There, on the morning of her company's gala affair, her boss sought her out to say that he'd just reviewed the details of the party with the new public relations coordinator, and didn't like what he was seeing.

"You know how to give a good party," he said. "You know what I like too. Do it."

Jill could barely respond. She was a vice president, not someone's assistant. Her calendar was filled with important meetings, and she was well aware the boss would never have similarly commandeered a male employee. Additionally, she liked the new public relations person and knew that taking over her job would damage their relationship.

What did Jill do? She canceled the appointments she could, asked her peers to keep the ones that couldn't be postponed, and threw herself into planning the best party in the convention's history, all in ten hours. The reason: She knew that the boss was the team leader and that the party mattered to him. Even though planning the affair didn't fit her job description, she was aware that by doing it, and by doing it right, she was making herself an indispensable member of the team. She was also showing that the team was more important than her own ego.

The event was fabulous, and her boss, as well as the rest of her team, knew why.

Unfortunately, this story is the exception to the rule. Too many women I know worry so much about protecting their hard-won professional position—or their friends' territory—that they can forget about teamwork.

Boys learn that being part of a team means doing what the leader tells you to do, and shutting up about it. You can argue with the coach when he calls the play. You can point out mistakes. But once the play is in operation, you perform your assigned part to the best of your ability.

Women have little practice following a team leader because of the group orientation of our games. Our social circles, being democratic, made us think everyone was equal.

Consider the following: I recently phoned a department in my office to relay some sensitive information on a breaking story. The boss was on vacation, and the person who took the call was a new employee with little experience handling the kind of story I was reporting, and even less seasoning as a leader. When I asked to speak to the person in charge, she told me, "No one's in charge. We're doing this as a team effort."

I didn't have the time to talk to a group, and hung up. I wanted to talk to a leader. Finally I decided not to pass the tip along. Suppose my information was wrong? Who would check it? Who would give a final go-ahead? And who would be the spokesperson if we needed to do a postmortem? A team isn't a team without a leader.

THE PROBLEM: You're having trouble fitting in because business is a team sport.

WHAT TO DO: Remember that your job is not about you. It's about the team. You have to follow team rules:

Play with the big picture in mind: It isn't your job to feel insulted if a particular task seems beneath you. If the situation warrants immediate attention, no one wants to hear about your personal doubts. Your individual concerns, no matter how important to you, are the small picture. The big picture is the team's ability to score a goal. You've been hired because you can contribute to the team. That means you can't get caught up in minutiae or waste energy disliking people or worrying about your own problems.

You don't have to like your teammates, but you do have to stay loyal to them: Regard the least-capable member of your team as a problem to solve, and not a personal affront. A team is only as good as its weakest link. Strengthen that link and you strengthen yourself.

You don't have to think of yourself as an automaton: Unique, interesting, unusual, different—these words describe a woman's charm. They make us attractive to our partners and to the world. So it's easy to think that if you become a team player, you'll become invisible. You won't. In fact, you'll become a better version of you. A good center can help make a good quarterback look great; a good catcher improves a pitcher; all good doubles partners help each other. Each member of your team brings his or her own unique talents to the playing field; you can improve yours by taking advantage of all the talents around you.

Don't second guess the team: As we saw in Chapter 3: Learn the Playing Field, once a team decision has been made, it's time to move on. There is no move called *Pause,* or *Stop and Think About It*, or, worse, *Second Guess*. I've often made this mistake, and have often been reprimanded. The most common situation: The boss and I are going out to lunch, and after we make a decision where to go, I bring up all the other alternatives—whereas all my boss wants to do is eat.

If you want your team to score a goal, it's not helpful to keep proposing alternative ideas. When everyone on the team is running to the left, this isn't the moment to ask if it wouldn't be better to run to the right.

Examine your internal conversation: Write down your complaints about work and read them aloud. Are they all I—and me—oriented? Many of you will think, "Not me." But we can be very egotistical, in ways that we don't always recognize.

Say, for example, you have an incompetent co-worker, so you wrote, "I think he's a jerk." "He never listens to anything I say." "He's not as smart as I am." Do you see the egotism in that impulse? We become so wrapped up in our negative energy, so convinced that if someone would just listen to us everything would improve, that we can end up obsessed with a team member who's not sharp.

Rather than sound off, pitch in and help. Find a way to make positive suggestions. Devote your critical talents to making the team work better instead of just criticizing. Never approach the team leader with only a complaint. Have a solution handy as well.

Let the team help you: When we get frustrated with our teammates and say, "I can do it better and quicker myself," we usually make a strategic mistake—as well as take on too much work.

As tempting as it may seem to transgress boundaries, don't. A center fielder doesn't try to pitch, a goalie doesn't try to score. If you really think you could do someone else's job better than he or she can, go to the team leader and discuss it confidentially.

It's a very female tendency to undertake more than our share, and one that I believe evolves from being a mother. You can put the dishes away twice as fast as your child, so you don't ask her to do it. But if you never give her the opportunity to try, even if it takes her extra time, how will she learn?

Fact: Many women fail because they can't accept help. You see them in their offices at 7:30 P.M., doing the work of five other people—people who have long since gone home. When questioned, they explain that instructing the people under them seemed too laborious and, furthermore, by the time they were done teaching, they could have done the actual job better and quicker.

But the result of your doing too much is that you become angry, and your employees don't learn anything. Worse: In the end, because you can't do it all yourself, you eventually fail. That's the reason you have a team in the first place.

Don't torpedo the team: Perhaps the worst play we make as a team player is to forget we're on the team. Yes, there are many other items on your agenda every day—the house, the relationship, the kids, the parents, and so on. But while you're at work, except in time of real personal crisis, your prime objective is the team's success. I'm not saying the rest of your life isn't important, but if you want to be successful, focus on your work while you're at work.

When you need time off to take care of a serious personal problem, ask for it. If your company is so rigid that it can't accommodate an urgent personal need, you're probably in the wrong place.

. . . . .

12 | Don't Assume Responsibility Without Authority

SITUATION: The boss is upset because a key department is underperforming.

HIS MOVE: If persuaded to help out, he makes sure that the boss gives him the authority to tackle the problem.

HER MOVE: She immediately volunteers to help, and her offer is accepted. Happy that her boss has such confidence in her, she never asks for the appropriate authority.

Consider Jill, who threw that big party even though it wasn't in her bailiwick as a vice president. Before Jill canceled her scheduled appointments, before she asked her associates to see the clients she couldn't postpone, before she threw herself into planning the best party in the convention's history, she told her boss that she needed the authority to run the event as she saw fit: to spend what had to be spent, to hire the people who needed to be hired. She couldn't keep coming back to the boss every time she ran into an obstacle. The people who had been working on the party needed to know she was in charge.

Her boss agreed. And he made it clear that by accepting this condition, she was prepared to take the heat if the party were a flop. Jill was smart enough to accept this as good news, knowing that if the party was a success, she'd get the credit.

Having responsibility without the necessary authority is one of the prime issues women face in business.

Say the boss is in a quandary—there's a problem in the creative end, and he knows that the guy in charge, Jack, isn't getting things done. He calls a meeting of his trusted inner circle to discuss the situation. By the time the meeting is over, you've volunteered to help Jack out. You haven't been offered a new job or been given new responsibility or received more money. You're just "helping."

Most guys know that each position comes with a specific responsibility. A goalie protects the goal, a quarterback throws the ball. The object is to win, and everyone plays his specific role to move the team to victory.

Because so many of us feel, correctly, that it's hard to get noticed on our merits, women break this rule over and over. We take on responsibility after responsibility because we want to show that we have a variety of talents, because we believe that we should always be congenial and willing to do anything.

But taking on any job without obtaining the proper authority wastes time as well as emotional and intellectual energy. You're trying to finish off a task in an area where the key people don't report to you. Instead of looking like a problem solver, you look like an interloper. The boss is standing above the fray, clean and distant, while you're in there, sleeves rolled up, taking charge of a group of people who resent your presence, who don't know if you're a permanent threat, and who are unclear about the status of their old boss.

It's a potential morass. You remember the boss's last words to you: "I want you to know that whenever you open your mouth, you are speaking for me." Do these words help now?

No. Because unless the top person gives you authority officially and publicly, you don't really have it. And responsibility without authority creates confusion, unhappiness, and trouble.

THE PROBLEM: You've volunteered to help the boss so often you're overextended and the lines of authority at your company have become unclear.

WHAT TO DO: Don't volunteer next time. Stifle your impulses. You're not there to make everything okay and your boss knows it.

The truth is that a woman is more likely to initiate the dreaded responsibility-without-authority problem than her boss is. He doesn't really expect us to solve his problem—not unless we've volunteered so often he takes our participation for granted.

Believe me, I know how hard it is not to offer help. I still have to restrain myself. But what I finally understood was that when a male boss complains about a bad situation, he usually just wants to vent.

Say he tells you that old Jim is doing a bad job in the accounting department, that he can't get along with his employees, that there's constant turnover. We are so trained to be caretakers that instead of saying, "Yes, I understand, that sounds difficult," we offer, "Jim and I have a great relationship. Do you want me to talk to him?"

No, no, no. The boss didn't expect you to take action. He probably won't turn down the offer— why should he? It won't cost him. But he wasn't asking. He was whining.

Offer your services only when are you certain that the task is a career opportunity. But be clear that you're making a trade-off. I never knew a volunteer in this kind of circumstance who didn't end up feeling exploited. Her boss started taking her goodwill for granted, and by the time she either became furious with him, or realized how over-extended she was, it was too late. So instead of becoming the boss's favored pet and improving her prospects, the relationship soured.

GAME HINT: At different times, nearly all men will treat almost all women as though we're subordinate. Be wary. If someone giving a presentation needs a drink of water, you can fetch it for him, but don't leave the impression that you're *always* the one responsible for water.

I know one female executive who says she loves to get the water or coffee for clients because it shows that she's not as self-important as her male colleagues, and the speakers always remember her fondly. But if you're worried about looking subordinate, whisper or hand a note to the person closest to the water pitcher that the speaker needs a drink.

Likewise, you needn't volunteer to take notes at every meeting. No law says that a woman has to be the secretary. If you do it once, suggest that, in the future, the task should rotate around the table, and note in your minutes who's next in line to take over. But don't become so dogmatic that you seem uncooperative or defensive. Find a way to make these tasks everyone's responsibility.

13 | Sit at the Table

SITUATION: The boss has called a big meeting in the conference room. There are ten chairs at the table, and another two dozen by the wall.

HIS MOVE: He sits at the table.

HER MOVE: She sits by the wall.

Imagine this scenario: The team is on the field at practice, and suddenly there's an open position.

Four players are sitting on the bench. One of them is sticking his hands in the coach's face, begging to get in. The other three are ducking behind each other.

It's a scenario you'll never see, because a major part of playing the game is being ready to run out on the field. When the coach wants you, you're available. You're always fully present and accounted for.

The classic office equivalent is the meeting in the conference room, where there always seem to be fewer chairs around the table than people to sit in them. The rest of the chairs are by the wall, or at one end of the room, or directly behind the boss's throne.

Women often take those peripheral chairs, because we think that the table is for the boss and the key people, or those who would be disgruntled sitting anywhere else. In other words, the men.

It's time that we realize that if we want to be considered loyal and productive team players, we have to sit at the table with the Big Guys.

The power with which a person presents herself is quite different if she is sitting at the table or at the far end of the room next to the bookcases. No matter how great your knowledge, sitting in the bleachers makes you look subordinate. The boss is far less apt to ask for your opinion if he has to shift in his seat to see you and strain his ears to hear you.

. . . . .

THE PROBLEM: You feel uncomfortable sitting at the table, particularly when there aren't enough chairs for everyone.

WHAT TO DO: The difference between you and that guy who scurried past you to sit in a prime location is self-confidence.

Early on guys learn that they belong at the table, and they're comfortable fighting to stay there. Being visible is half the battle. You can't play if you can't be seen.

Don't let a lack of self-confidence damage your career. Catch yourself: Are you thinking that only the big shots can sit at the boss's table? Are you thinking that you're taking the place of someone smarter? What if you're asked to contribute, and you're exposed as an imposter?

To circumvent these hurtful thoughts, women often pretend it doesn't matter where we sit. Scores of them have told me that if it makes the guys so happy, why fight? To defer on this point becomes a badge of honor—we don't need to show off.

It's not showing off. It's making your presence felt—and you should come to work every day fully present.

This isn't to say you should just grab whatever seat you can at a regular weekly meeting. People may have customary places at the table and such a move could be perceived as an obnoxious power play. But you'll go to many meetings with no de facto assigned seats, meetings where your knowledge is as important as anyone else's. When that happens, simply gather your confidence, march up to the table, and sit.

GAME HINT: Take your place at the table, metaphorically speaking, in every aspect of work. For instance, at a company party, don't let the guys monopolize the clients. The boss is constantly looking around the room to see who's moving the ball, and if he sees you ensconced in the corner, safe and comfortable with a friend, you lose points.

Make your presence known everywhere. At a business lecture for a hundred people, for example, sit in the first few rows of the auditorium. We walk into these rooms as though we were attending a distant friend's wedding and a back row seat is the best we deserve. Instead, make it a rule to act like a member of the wedding party rather than a guest.

By sitting in the front row, you'll make contact with the speaker and the subject matter, too. When you sit on the periphery, you take in a peripheral amount of information. In the front row, you're forced to listen.

At the same time, you'll be getting used to the limelight. Co-workers will see you up front and will be persuaded to reconsider their image of you.

. . . . .

Keep in mind: If there are twelve seats at the table, and traditionally two of those have belonged to women, don't feel that you have to sit in one of them. Don't get caught in the trap of competing only for what is seen as a woman's place, job, or title. We won't try out for every position on the team until we believe that every position can be ours.

14|Laugh

Situation: It's a tough meeting, and the tension in the room is thick. Then one of the guys tells a joke—it's not very funny, and most everyone has heard it before.
His move: He laughs.
Her move: She doesn't.

Laugh. Grin. Smile: anything—anything at all. Guys learned long ago that humor can cut the tension in any situation.

Unfortunately for us, the kind of wise-cracking, back-slapping, knee-smacking humor that breaks the guys up is seldom the kind we've learned to enjoy. Our humor leans more toward the observational, the situational. What's more, we don't tend to joke with each other the way men do—at least, not when we're growing up. We don't even learn to initiate jokes. I remember once hearing comedian

Phyllis Diller say that the major problem she had breaking into stand-up comedy was that all the bookers told her flat out, "Women can't tell a joke."

Think about it. We're much more likely to giggle about that strange-looking guy who monopolized the boss's wife at the office party than we are to announce when we have something to say and demand everyone's attention. And in a tough meeting at the office, pithy little observations don't always cut it.

Of course, there are a great deal of not-so-humorous men, but for the most part they can still tell a joke to break the tension. I have met few women who can do that.

It's not really our fault. We can be so focused on doing a good job, so concerned with showing the guys we can do the work, that we're not relaxed enough to introduce a little levity.

We also don't realize that the laughing has less to do with telling the actual joke than with creating camaraderie. When you read about a retired football player reminiscing about the game, you understand it's not the plays or the noise of the crowd he misses—it's the friendship.

THE PROBLEM: The guys at the office think women are too driven, too serious, to have a sense of humor.

WHAT TO DO: Don't take yourself too seriously.

As former Washington Redskins football player John Riggins once said to Supreme Court Justice Sandra Day O'Connor at a formal dinner, "Loosen up, Sandy baby." Just because you don't know how to tell a joke a guy's way doesn't mean you can't be funny and engaging. So maybe you don't get the big belly laugh. At least your male colleagues won't mutter that you're another humorless female. I don't think anyone who is totally humorless can make it high up the ladder.

I know I'm not a joke teller and never will be, but whenever I do get a laugh, the guys come up to me later with a surprised expression and say, "I didn't realize that you were funny." They say it as though I were a newly discovered subspecies: Homo Sapiens, Female Humorous.

There's one man I've worked with for years who, every time I make him smile, says, "You were funny again." That in itself has become our little running joke. (I said these jokes can be small, as long as you're a part of them.)

Even if you can't tell a funny story, let your associates know you appreciate theirs. Sometimes that may mean laughing at things you don't find very humorous. But if you're a mother, think how many times you've laughed at one of your child's terrible jokes. I must have heard the same knock-knock jokes a thousand times. And I always laugh at them, because I love my kids and grandkids and I know it's important they feel my approval.

If you're going to be a spoilsport, people won't feel comfortable around you. Yet all you had to do was smile pleasantly when someone told you a joke, even if you heard it four times before.

GAME HINT: Dirty jokes. No for both sexes. When women try to be humorous in a quasi-locker room kind of way, we usually end up making ourselves, and the guys, uneasy. I've yet to hear a female colleague tell a good off-color joke. This may change, but for the time being, if it's tough for a woman to tell a joke, it's almost impossible for her to tell a dirty joke. There is too much sexual tension, too many rules, too much political correctness in the workplace. The guys who have known me for years are always asking me what topics to avoid when they talk to female associates they don't know well. The one thing I recommend: Stay away from anything with sexual overtones.

6

SIX THINGS MEN CAN DO AT WORK THAT WOMEN CAN'T

To be somebody, a woman does not have to be more like a man, but has to be more of a woman.
DR. SALLY E. SHAYWITZ, PHYSICIAN AND WRITER

THERE'S A FAMOUS DUET IN THE MUSICAL *Annie Get Your Gun* sung by Annie Oakley and her friendly competitor Frank Butler called "Anything You Can Do, I Can Do Better." In the context of business, that song could be retitled "Anything You Can Do, I Can Do Too, with Dire Consequences."

In professional sports, a NOT WELCOME sign still greets women. We're allowed to become fans, we're allowed to become journalists, we're even allowed to own the franchise. But although few sports have rules that specifically prohibit us from playing, we haven't been invited to join the team, yet.

In business, the NOT WELCOME sign came down a few decades ago, but that doesn't mean that women are always well-received once we get in the door. We're not. Just as the first woman major league baseball player will be assessed differently, and more harshly, than a male, we are being rigorously scrutinized for everything we do that doesn't jibe with what men expect businesspeople to do. We're judged by male standards, not our own, which means men can take certain actions freely that we cannot.

This doesn't mean that we can't cry when we don't get promoted, have an affair with a co-worker, yell at our secretary, and so on. We just can't cry, or have an affair, or yell, and expect the same consequences as a man. We will pay a high price, our place in the game will shift, people's perception of us will change.

The other day I read an article about a powerful businesswoman who said that, once she'd reached a certain level of power, she told the men around her that she always cried when she became upset or angry and that they were just going to have to get used to it. She didn't care if it made them uncomfortable. She didn't want to stifle her instinct any longer. Let the tears flow.

As you'll read below, crying is one of the many actions that are judged differently in a woman and a man. But if you fully understand the consequences of these kinds of actions, and you feel that you can use them to your advantage, then by all means, go ahead and fidget, cry, yell—to your heart's content.

1 | They Can Cry. You Can't

When former U.S. senator Lauch Faircloth of North Carolina lost his reelection bid, tears stained his cheeks at his press conference. The media called this a powerful display of emotion. When former congresswoman and then-presidential candidate Pat Schroeder cried on television, men smirked. Just like a woman, they said.

Men can get away with tears because it's unexpected. Men believe powerful people don't cry. If they do, they must have an excellent reason.

Women are expected to cry. And when we do, men think it's because we're giving in to a natural instinct or worse, they think we're using tears as a game prop, a tool to manipulate them into feeling guilt.

Many years ago I knew a man who was fired from a rival media company. He marched into his boss's office and burst into tears, telling the boss that he could never disclose to his wife what had happened because she looked up to him, that he could no longer afford to keep his kids in private school, that he'd have to drop out of his private club.

The boss's reaction? He felt terrible—not because the guy didn't need to be fired (the move was long overdue), but because the boss could see himself in the same situation. "Here's a breadwinner just like me," he thought. "What would happen if I were in his shoes? Would I fall apart like this?"

The boss called Human Resources and gave the man six additional months of severance.

A month later, that same boss fired a woman. When she cried in the office, he was so uncomfortable that the moment she left, he walked out and told a colleague, "We were right to let her go. Can you believe she broke down right in my office? I don't want people working for us who can't control their emotions."

2 | They Can Have Sex. You Can't

A woman at a major accounting firm once confided in me, "One of the major reasons I've succeeded is that there are so few sexy men here. I was never tempted."

Not a small point. I always recommend that unless they're outright husband hunting, job seekers look for positions in places where they find the men generally unattractive.

Some companies are fraught with sexual tension, whether the employees are attractive or not. You feel it from the moment you walk in the door for your first interview. You see it in the way people look at each other. You hear it in the suggestive comments.

Avoid these places. They're the ones where you're likely to get caught up in a sexual liaison. And when you do, you lose.

Men are more likely to get away with sex in the office. The reason? After the romance is gone and the fighting starts, the more powerful person plots to oust the subordinate from the picture. Since a man is generally the one with the clout, the woman usually ends up getting fired, transferred, or pushed aside. Little if anything happens to him.

Even if a woman ends her affair without a demotion, she's still tarred. People will always see her differently; they'll say her success is due to her sexual skills. And without her team's respect, she's not a desirable player.

For a man, the worst-case scenario (apart from dismissal) is a sexual harassment suit. But to win her case a woman has to prove that sex wasn't con-sensual, and that might be hard to do after a two-year fling.

GAME STUDY: Not long ago one of the top-ranking women at a large manufacturing conglomerate left her job for a smaller company on the opposite coast. The official reason: She had the long-term potential of making serious money. The real reason: She had been having an affair with a married vice president and got caught. The two had been equals within the hierarchy, which is one reason the woman felt she was safe when the romance started. She knew it wouldn't last forever, and when it ended, she figured they would both return to the life they knew before.

What she hadn't counted on was office gossip. At her level, there were three other women and 25 men. She had told only one of the women, but somehow all the men seemed to know. Her former lover denied he'd told a soul, and it didn't really matter whether he was telling the truth or not. The damage was done. If the subject of extramarital sex arose, every man in the room would look directly at her. Any time anyone made a sexual joke, any time sexual innuendo pervaded the air, she always felt it referred to her. At company social events many of the men began to come on to her as if she were sexually available.

Perhaps she was oversensitive, or perhaps the men really were making her life miserable. Regardless, she knew she felt too uncomfortable to achieve the results she wanted, so she left.

3 | They Can Fidget. You Can't

A close friend who works at a huge software concern told me this story: While he was sitting in a meeting with one woman and seven other men, the woman, a rising star, occasionally tapped her fingernails on her watch, making a sharp clicking sound. Every time she did this, at least one man shot her a look. These looks weren't kind. And they meant that for that one moment he wasn't paying attention to the meeting, but to her.

About an hour into the meeting one of the men, another star, began drumming his fingers on the table. Since everyone in the room had seen this behavior before, they knew what it meant: The man was becoming bored. Because he was well regarded, his impatience infected the rest of the room, and the meeting quickly broke up.

Women fidget. Tapping our fingers, twirling our hair, smoothing our dress usually represents an old habit from childhood, and usually indicates insecurity.

Personally, I had a habit of pushing my cuticles back with my fingers. I kept my hands in my lap as I did it, so I figured no one could see me. But years ago a male executive asked me brusquely why an executive would do something so silly. I immediately stopped. I was startled that anyone had ever seen me do it.

Guys consider a woman's annoying little habits exactly that—annoying little habits. To them, she's broadcasting to the world that she is uncomfortable, insecure, flustered.

When a man is tapping, however, it usually means he's impatient. Thus it tends to be a power play, a nonverbal cue that says, "I'm bored, I've heard enough of this, let's get it over with."

If you want to play the game the way men play, don't do anything that makes them think less of you. If you do, you are letting your power erode.

GAME HINT: As you go up the corporate ladder, you'll have more of an opportunity to sit in those huge, overstuffed chairs in presidents' offices and boardrooms. They're so large they'll make you feel like a kid again. I've seen important women sit in one of those chairs and suddenly start fidgeting like a twelve-year-old.

Sadly, office furniture is built for men. The manufacturers have no choice but to make those chairs male-sized, which means they are usually uncomfortable for us. Instead of being fully present, with our hands in front of us and our back erect, the chair seems too low, the table too high; when you try to fidget your way to comfort, the table seems too low, the chair too high. It's hard to feel powerful when your feet barely touch the ground.

Learn how to sit in a man's world. It's his equipment, his furniture. To look as though you're in command of the space you inhabit, try some simple tricks. Don't let the space command you. Lean forward, sit on the edge of the chair, be present. When you find a place of comfort, stay there. I have to admit it took me years to figure out how to inhabit my executive desk chair.

Someday we may have the power to design our own furniture. It's hard to imagine, but try to picture the moment when office furniture is tailored for women's bodies, and it's the men who are fidgeting to find comfort.

4 | They Can Yell. You Can't

Recently two executives, a man and a woman, engaged in a public fight in the corridors of CNN. Within the space of ten minutes, the story came back to me through several different people, which meant it was moving rapidly around the building. I know that the woman became very angry and finally called the man a prick. I know that he called her something equally bad.

I don't know exactly what else he said, or he did, because all the reports of the story concerned her. This woman had yelled just as loudly and as furiously as the man. People were astounded.

No one is surprised to hear a man raise his voice, see him show his anger publicly, watch him turn red and fume. Men are expected to shout. They spend their lives roaring at each other. When they play games, they yell at their opponents, they yell at their teammates, they yell at the spectators. They yell at themselves, too.

Women, however, are taught to control our anger. When we feel upset, wronged, hurt, we learn to internalize it. Guys turn it outward; they blame whatever it was that made them angry, not themselves. Current statistics show that self-mutilation among American women is on the rise, and if you combine that with the figures on anorexia and bulimia, you see how much we direct our anger inwards.

When a woman does display anger, people are often uneasy, frightened; they perceive her as difficult, unladylike. They act as though she has no right to yell. After all, the woman's role is to work out issues in relationships, to mediate, to compromise.

Because men perceive a show of anger as something out of character for a woman, they judge it as a loss of control. It's almost always perceived negatively.

However, as I've accumulated more power, I've realized that there are times when a careful dose of yelling is appropriate. You can't keep inspiring people when they make mistakes or when they don't reach their goals if you don't occasionally vent your disappointment loudly and clearly. There's a point where people actually expect to be chastised, and a point where they'll stop trying hard unless external force is applied. That force is often a boss's wrath.

But I'm very cautious when I engage my anger. If a woman becomes angry too often, she will be seen as (what other word is there?) a bitch. For us, anger is at best used as a secret weapon, one that should be used sparingly and strategically.

You have a perfect right to get mad at someone. But when you do, take a deep breath, consider what you want to say, and say it in a controlled manner. This way you will display your self-possessed power rather than your lack of control.

GAME HINT: If you show some well-thought-out, justified anger, don't let your natural instinct for peace drive you to apologize later. When we get angry and punish our children, we rarely apologize if we felt we were right. The same goes for work. If the anger is genuine, express it, get over it quickly, and move on. Don't place yourself in a one-down position by expressing regrets.

5 | They Can Have Bad Manners. You Can't

When my daughter was 14 years old, I sent her to a four-day etiquette course. Some of what she learned was surely unnecessary—after all, how often is she going to curtsey to the Queen of England? If she has to, however, she'll be ready.

But much of the course was about the basic rules of behavior, because any woman who can't handle herself appropriately in every social situation faces a disadvantage. A man doesn't have to know which spoon to use, or how to cover a burp, or when to send a thank-you note. If he makes a mistake, he gets away with it, especially if he is considered powerful.

Consider: On a recent episode of television's *Frasier*, Frasier Crane's brother, Niles, hires a powerful attorney to handle his divorce. In his first scene, the lawyer changes from his sweaty workout clothes into his suit in a thoroughly vulgar manner in front of both Crane brothers. The incident let the audience know the man was an excellent attorney, because anyone that gross, that ill-mannered, had to be talented.

Could a woman get away with that kind of behavior? Almost certainly not. It wouldn't be regarded as powerful. It would be regarded as repulsive. He's allowed to be rude, crude, and lewd. She's not.

Think about what happens after the guys win a game—they go out for a celebratory dinner and pig out. The coolest guy at the table is the one who eats and drinks the most and has the worst manners. The guy who sits calmly with his napkin in his lap, slowly sipping his beer and using a knife and fork, is considered a spoilsport.

Women are rewarded for neat homework, proper etiquette, good penmanship. We are called "good girls" if we're well-groomed and well-behaved. Guys who are too well-groomed and well-behaved are called something else.

Whether we're going to the White House or meeting with a local official, we like knowing how to do it right. The fine points are important. Making a faux pas causes us to question our self-image, our competence, our identity.

What was most interesting about the course my daughter took was the composition of the students. I had expected young Southern debutantes, and indeed there was a spattering of them. But there were also four grown women—two secretaries, a businesswoman, and a young doctor. When I asked them why they had come, the secretaries said that, because their bosses were of the old school, they needed to know how to handle both social and professional situations appropriately. The doctor said that, as a physician, she knew she'd have to deal with difficult senior colleagues and complex political scenarios. She didn't want to make a wrong move that could hinder her climb through the hospital hierarchy. And the businesswoman said that because most of her peers in middle management had attended fancy colleges or came from wealthy families, they knew how to negotiate a privileged world. She wasn't prepared to forfeit a promotion because she didn't know how to throw a dinner party.

6 | They Can Be Ugly. You Can't

When my friend Joan gave an address at a conference last month, she and her fellow female speakers were amused to see that one of the panel members was a middle-aged man whose pants were short enough to expose several inches of pale skin. Not only that, his socks were so stretched out they'd fallen down over his shoes, which were in turn horribly scuffed.

Imagine Joan's chagrin when she noticed on the way to the podium that she had a run in her stocking. It didn't show, she thought. But after her speech, when she dashed back to her hotel room to change, she overheard a woman in the back of the elevator ask a friend if she'd seen that poor woman who gave her presentation with that terrible run.

Just as they get away with social mistakes, men are likely to enjoy immunity from errors in their physical appearance—stained ties, missing buttons, mismatched socks. But no woman, no matter how important, seems to escape censure for even the tiniest sartorial flaw. It's as though such a lapse were a sign that she doesn't know, or doesn't care, or doesn't pay attention to details.

Actually, it's nothing but a sign that she has a

run in her stocking. (Frankly, the way stockings and panty hose are produced makes it difficult for any woman to conduct business life with dignity—but that's another topic.) We just don't get cut that kind of slack.

The worst part is, it's not just men who judge us so harshly. We do it to each other (remember the women in the elevator).

GAME HINT: It's not only our clothes that make people so judgmental. It can be anything: our looks, our weight, our breath.

For example, I don't think anyone does well with body odor or bad breath. But I've done business with plenty of men who are offensive on both counts, and no one has ever mentioned it. Yet I know a mid-level female executive with bad breath whose company decided she was unpromotable. Apparently, none of her peers wanted to work on her committees or attend her meetings. (I imagine she suffered from some kind of metabolic dysfunction, but no one knew how to broach the subject.)

What holds for breath, holds for weight. Despite some enormous advances in their consciousness, men still seem to believe that every woman wants to be thin. And if she isn't, they assume she must have poor self-control, a problem which they fear could slip over into her work.

However, men who are fat are often able to

present their girth as a sign of their importance and prosperity. One well-known Hollywood producer uses his immense body (which he covers with garish disheveled clothes) to suggest that he's so powerful he doesn't have to pay attention to his appearance. And as long as he really is a major player, this approach works. (The moment he starts losing power, however, I'll bet he cleans up his act.)

7

HE HEARS, SHE HEARS: TEN GENDERBENDER VOCABULARY WORDS

*Show me a woman who doesn't feel guilty
and I'll show you a man.*
ERICA JONG, WRITER AND FEMINIST

WHILE WRITING THIS BOOK I INTERVIEWED BOTH men and women, and in our conversations I noticed different interpretations of the word *rules*. The men assumed I was writing down an absolute code for women to follow, a specific set of instructions. For them, the rules of the game are exactly that: rules.

The first things a guy asks when he plays a game: Who goes first? How do you keep score? How long does it last? Unless the man thinks of himself as a rebel, in which case he can break all the rules, he plays by them. Men rarely assume that rules bend.

The women I talked to, however, thought of rules as guidelines, hints, suggestions—exactly as I do. When girls play a game, they're more likely to ask: Can my friend play too? Can we make the game last a little longer? I have to do an errand for my mother, can I come back in half an hour?

Women want to have a relationship with the rules. When necessary, we'll consider adapting them to each personal situation we find ourselves in. For instance, if the rule says to play a game with five people on each side for two 30-minute segments, we'll ask if we can break for dinner, or extend the game into the next day, or add two people to each side, or play with a large ball instead of a small one. (Ten guys would play for an hour, total.)

To accommodate an unforeseen event, to prevent a teammate from getting her feelings hurt, to include as many as possible, we are comfortable rewriting the rules as the situation warrants.

In fact, as soon as I put my ideas down on paper, I knew that I would rethink some of them. When I told that to a male co-worker, he looked horrified. "You can't change your rules just because you feel like it," he said. The word *rules* has a different meaning for men and women.

Over the years I've come upon ten other words that men and women define differently. They are:

. . . . .

1|Yes (Exactly What It Means)

Some years ago I was in a large, disorganized meeting where several people were vigorously pressing their agendas. Perhaps most agitated was one woman who needed to increase her department's budget.

Arriving in the room fully prepared, her briefcase bulging with folders, her notepad overflowing with handwritten notes, she started her presentation forcefully and wasn't more than a minute into it when her boss interrupted. "You're right," he said. "You can have what you need."

The woman paused briefly, and then continued her speech. The boss interrupted again: "I said, yes."

The woman pressed on.

"I said, yes," the boss repeated—to no avail. The woman continued. The boss threw up his hands. "Okay," he said, "I've changed my mind. The answer is no. Now will you stop talking?"

I'm constantly struck by how often a woman goes into a meeting, asks for something she thinks she won't get, receives a favorable reply—and continues to pitch.

Yes means *yes*—no matter how much time and energy you've put into preparing for a *no*.

I always think of a woman receiving the ultimate affirmation—"I love you, will you marry me?"—and responding: "Do you really mean it? Are you sure? Did I pressure you into saying it? When did you realize your feelings? What is it about me you like most?"

Why do we do this? One reason is that when we were younger, many of us learned intricate ways to manipulate people. If we wanted Dad or Mom to let us date a new guy or attend that party across town, for example, we had to be circular and protracted, forever restating our position to get the desired reply.

Business isn't family. When you get what you want, take it and shut up.

Another complicating factor: Many women in business are constantly on guard against being patronized. We don't want the boss to cave just because we're the only woman in the room and he has no choice but to say yes. We want him to hear our cogent, unimpeachable argument from start to finish, and decide we're right. We want him to *want* to agree.

Once again, it's a relationship issue: A woman sees two people, boss and employee, and she's hoping to reach a consensus based on shared mutual sensibilities rather than get an impersonal response—even a positive one. We want the feeling of validation. The man, however, wants a favorable response.

In school, you may have gotten someone to agree with you because you were friendly, because everyone liked you, because you were smart. In business, if you're getting a *yes*, it isn't because people find you so appealing. It's because your idea makes sense.

2|No (Not What It Means)

As we saw in Chapter 5: Make a Request (and it bears repeating): Women consider *no* one of the most fearsome words in the language. When we were ten years old, we would hear the word *no* and melt in tearful drama—"If you won't let me sleep over at Jennie's house, she'll never want to be my friend again"!

Consider this example: A young woman recently entered my office in tears. She was trying to convince her boss to give her a new project under development, and he had said, no, it was the wrong time to ask. That's all he said—the wrong time. But the woman was completely deflated. She had been convinced her idea was good; now she never wanted to mention her idea again. Her confidence was in shreds. In her mind, weeks of planning had come to nothing.

"Wait a minute," I said. "He just said the timing was bad. He probably had 30 other things to think about and your project wasn't one of them. He was only telling you to come back another day." It took me almost an hour to convince her.

Because we equate *no* with a crushing defeat, we often frame questions to prepare us for rejection. For example, "I don't suppose that you would consider . . . ?" Or, "Could you possibly let me . . . ?" Or, "Is there any chance in the world that I could . . . ?"

Just the other day I heard a woman approach her boss after a meeting and ask, "Is there any chance at all, given that I'm not really qualified, and that other people have probably already asked, that you might consider letting me work on your new project?"

When the boss turned her down, she nodded in agreement. It was as if she and he were now on the same side: Neither of them really felt she was the right person.

Once again: *No* simply means that whatever you asked for—at that time, of that person, in that way—didn't materialize. It has nothing to do with whether you're bright and talented and will ultimately succeed. Says my younger son, the president of a California outsourcing company, "I love the word *no*. For me, it is the first step to thinking strategically how to convince my boss or my client to get to a yes."

3 | Hope (The Worst Word in the Game)

"I hope everyone reading this book profits from it." "I hope this book does well." "I hope I write another."

If I ever say those sentences aloud, please shoot me.

Hope is one of the most unempowering words in the English language. Why? Because it allows us to believe we're taking action, when, in reality, we're taking no action at all.

Little girls are brought up to believe that all we have to do is sit still, smile, be smart, act charming, and the world will arrive on our doorsteps, whether that means being asked to the prom by the handsomest boy in school, or being elected the first female president of the United States. It's as though we were all Cinderellas, waiting for our fairy godmothers to grant us our wishes.

Little boys dream, too. But their upbringing teaches them that dreaming is not enough. Even as a twelve-year-old is imagining he's hitting the winning home run, he's learning the moves. He is practicing every day, he is memorizing the playbook, he is imagining the feel of connecting the bat to the ball.

In a little girl's fantasy play, in the stories she reads, in the way she talks with her friends, she imagines being done to, rather than doing; she's passive rather than active.

I see this pattern day after day in the office and on the road. Recently I was in St. Louis talking to a large gathering of young journalists. Afterwards, 20 aspiring women approached me and handed me their cards, all saying that they dreamed about having a job like mine. Was there any possibility . . . ?

I showed interest in these women's ambitions. I encouraged them to write. I told them if they were really serious about new jobs, they should start strategizing and get in touch with me. I then flew back to Atlanta, knowing from experience that it would be unusual if I heard from just one of these women. In fact, I didn't hear from any of them.

Did they think that by handing me their card, I would search them out at whatever newspaper or television station they worked, and presto! turn them into a news correspondent?

When a man hustles me about a job, I can almost always count on hearing from him again. If I don't, I assume it's because he's found something else.

What will it take for women to give ourselves permission to do more than hope? The word we should be using is *want*, the word that the men use. Not "I hope," but, "I want." "I want that job." "I want to make that salary." "I want to become a manager."

When you say aloud that you want something, you give your thought power. It's the first step to getting your plan off the ground.

Like the fairy tales in which they appear, words like *hope* and *wish* are full of magic. But business and life aren't magical. Recently I sat on a panel

with four successful women. When asked their for-
mulas for success, every one of them replied, "I
work harder and smarter than everyone else."

Success isn't about wishing and praying and
hoping that someone will make you successful. It's
about deciding that you want to be successful, and
then making it happen.

4 | Guilt (It Means Trouble)

My dictionary defines guilt as "a painful feeling
of self-reproach resulting from a belief that one has
done something wrong." The entry is not illus-
trated—the closest picture appears next to the word
guillotine—but if there were a picture, it could easily
be a shot of a female business executive.

We feel so guilty all the time. We are brought
up to be good girls, and then we allow ourselves to
become the victims of our own good intentions.
We want to be superwomen, able to do everything.
And when we fail, we feel devastated. We may as
well have gotten the guillotine.

Besides making you feel miserable, guilt impedes
your ability to function. How can you keep your eye
on your goal if you're constantly berating yourself
about insignificant details? There you are, in a late-
hours meeting discussing your company's next big
move, and you can't focus on the agenda because
nagging thoughts preoccupy you—you forgot to call

your parents, you didn't order the birthday cake, you didn't make that call to your college alumni association . . .

Think about it. Maybe you did forget a few things. We all do. Maybe you did make a mistake. We all do. So what?

A man at that meeting wouldn't worry, even if it was his responsibility to pick up a nice dinner on the way home and he won't have time. He knows his family won't starve, he knows that it's the big finish that matters. He won't allow himself to get bogged down in the little details. There's nothing wrong with going out for fast food if necessary.

The word *guilt* doesn't exist at all on the game field. As long as they play by the rules, the guys don't feel guilty because they won, or because they ran over the opposition. They keep their focus on the game and the game alone.

Just because you can't do everything right doesn't mean you do everything wrong. Give yourself a break. If you feel guilty every time life isn't perfect, you'll feel guilty all the time.

5 | Sorry (It's a Sorry Word)

A man tells a female co-worker that the coffee wagon is late, that he can't find his cell phone, that his son's softball team lost a big game, that the company is revising its profit forecasts downward, that he has to fire his assistant, that his boss is angry at him, that the world is coming to an end.

Her response to everything: I'm sorry.

The word *sorry* is a female addiction. We use it so often, to express so much, and in so many contexts, it has virtually no meaning. It's just something we say, the iceberg lettuce of conversation, a kind of verbal filler.

I know women who start and end almost every sentence with the word *sorry*. "I'm sorry but I have to ask you . . ." "I'm sorry to do this but . . ." or ". . . and I'm sorry about that." It's an attempt to form a connection with another person, even though for the most part, the other person doesn't hear us.

When we use *sorry*, we're seldom referring to something we did wrong. If that were the case, rather than mumble a weak apology, we should make a strong affirmative statement, one that explains why the error occurred, or how we can make up for it, or how to prevent it from happening again. When I'm really and truly sorry about something I did, I say that I deeply regret my actions, that I am truly concerned—but I never say, "I'm sorry."

When a guy hears *sorry*, he infers that you've made a mistake. Say your boss tells you how an associate ruined a sale and the company lost a contract. You search your mind for something soothing to say and end up with, "I'm sorry." You think you're being

nice. But he hears you apologizing for doing something wrong. "What's she sorry about?" he wonders.
"She had nothing to do with it. Or did she?"

Saying that you are sorry has nothing to do with
your ability to empathize with another person's
misfortune. In fact, it has so little meaning that it
almost implies that you are indifferent. No woman
could say "I'm sorry" as much as she does and feel
that much pain and still be a functioning human
being.

6 | Aggressive (It's Not Assertive)

Here is a common scenario: The boss is trying
to fill an important position. In the interview, a
male applicant boasts about his abilities, explains
why he's the best person for the job, and urges the
boss to pick him. After the man leaves, the boss
compliments him by calling him aggressive.

A woman comes in and similarly boasts about
herself, says she's the obvious choice, and pushes
for a decision to be made soon. The boss finds her
domineering, overbearing, difficult. After she
leaves, the boss criticizes her by calling her aggressive.

Aggressive is a complex word at the office: When
a guy applies the word *aggressive* to another man, he
means that he's bold and forceful, that he wants to
win, that he has the strength and capabilities to

achieve his goal. But when guys use the word to describe women, the definition changes. The woman becomes pushy, argumentative, domineering.

For a woman, *aggressive* implies hostility, meanness, ruthlessness, for both men and women. It's about self rather than ego. It's about conquering other people, rather than compromising with them.

In brief: Men reserve the positive connotations of the word for themselves; they apply the negative ones to us. They have relegated to us the word *assertive*, which is what we are allowed to be when we want to forge ahead. It's a weak runner-up.

If men need to be aggressive to succeed, why shouldn't we be allowed to be aggressive, too? By allowing the positive connotation of the word to apply only to men, we're taking away our potential power.

7 | Fight (It's Not a Pretty Word)

Jacob and Jeanne worked at the same large corporation for many years. They started their careers at about the same time, and both ended up as vice presidents.

Like any other successful businessperson, Jacob's career has been laden with ups and downs, and he recently found himself in a particularly vulnerable political position. But he was confident he'd survive as he always had in the past until, when he least expected it, Jeanne attacked him from behind.

The reason? The two had engaged in a bitter turf war almost a decade earlier, one which Jeanne had been reluctant to enter. It became clear that Jacob was determined to duke it out, and in the end, he triumphed.

Once defeated, Jeanne seemed to acquiesce, and the former combatants returned peaceably to their work. But the truth was that Jeanne had never stopped plotting against Jacob. Finally, she found a way to hurt him irreparably.

Jacob had no idea the battle was still raging.

Attack. War. Battle. To a man, there's something—how else to put it?—manly in a good fight, something strong, dignified, something that has rules. You don't hit below the belt. You don't shoot someone in the back. You don't slug someone who's wearing glasses.

Men like to fight. They start fighting with each other when they're young, and they keep fighting until there's no fight left in them. Men fight while they're playing baseball, basketball, even while wearing the skates and heavy uniforms of hockey (Rodney Dangerfield's great line: The other night I went to a fight and a hockey game broke out). I know a nursing home attendant who says she has to break up fistfights between two octogenarians over rocking-space on the front porch.

Women avoid fighting at all costs. Every now and then I may have seen two girls slapping at each other, but for the most part, I can't ever remember seeing females brawling. Nor do I ever recall seeing girls fighting while playing a game. If you lost, if you were angry, the worst you did was huff and puff and storm away. If you were really mean, you took the ball or the board game with you.

But out-and-out fighting? Hardly. What if you hurt yourself? A boy with a black eye looks tough. A girl looks preternatural.

Because we don't see fighting as a sport, the concept of a fair fight is an oxymoron. A fight shouldn't take place. If it does, the rules go out the window. When a mother cat battles to save her kittens, there's no restraint in her behavior. She does whatever she can, including going in for the kill if necessary.

To a man, a fight is part of the game. One of you wins, one of you loses, and then the winner buys the loser a drink. You have to leave your opponent breathing, so you can play again.

Remember the next time you get into a fight with a male associate, while you're probably thinking of all-out warfare, he's only thinking of a temporary skirmish. And he's a lot more likely to enjoy the process than you are, which is all the more reason for you to get it over with quickly.

. . . . .

8 | Game (a.k.a.: Fun)

Maybe it's because *game* is a loaded word when it's applied to relationships. For example, "I just couldn't date Joey anymore. He was so into *games*." Maybe it's because we don't think we're as good at games as men. Maybe we feel that if we play a game with a man, we're expected to lose. But when we hear the word *game*, we get a little nervous.

Men are more likely to smile when they hear the word *game*. The word means something fun. When they play a game, they think they're going to win. What's not to like?

Here's a guy's secret: No one becomes a CEO by going through the motions. If you can't keep finding ways to maintain your enthusiasm for your job, you're going to get flat.

That's why guys have turned business into a game. It helps them devise new plays, invent new tactics, create new strategies to trounce their opponents. It allows them to have fun while they work.

I experience this phenomenon at work with my bookers and producers. Because they understand that business is a game, the truly excellent ones accept difficult challenges as part of their job description. They have fun dreaming up ways to do the completely impossible, they'll book the people no one else ever dreamed would be willing to appear on network television.

Thinking of work as a game is the best way to keep firm boundaries between you and your job. I know far too many women who are infuriated by their boss, or are irritated with a new colleague, or are haunted by an upcoming project, and who are unable to get away from the office because they can't stop wallowing in their unhappiness.

If you become mired in a tough situation, don't turn it into an emotional crisis. Instead, whenever you lose the contract or you don't get the promotion, funnel that unhappy energy into something more constructive, such as a new game plan that will lead you to success.

And remember that all games have a specific time limit. When they're over, they're over. So what if you lost? As soon as the next game starts, everyone is a possible victor once again. If you keep worrying about what went wrong with the last sale, you won't be ready for the next one.

9 | Glass Ceiling (Their Phrase, Not Ours)

A friend tells this story about her childhood. She, her older brother, and his friends would be playing cowboys and Indians, or cops and robbers. Most often she was the only girl. During the game, whenever she was doing well, her brother would shout out—"You're not allowed to go into the Forbidden Zone!" My friend never knew what the Forbidden Zone was, or why it appeared, but it always ruined her chances of winning. Because my friend was thrilled that the boys let her play, she lived with the rule; it was better than playing alone.

These days I'm often asked about the *glass ceiling*, and I want to shout, "There's no such thing as the Forbidden Zone!"

After all, isn't it possible the glass ceiling—some transparent barrier at the top of each corporation through which women can't pass—is purely a male invention? Do we accept it as a reality just because there are no women in the uppermost reaches? Maybe it's just a natural resting point we haven't figured out how to get beyond.

In the past women have broken through many of these "ceilings" and each time we do, the ceiling seems to have moved up. Once it was just above the vice president's job, then the executive vice president's, then the president's. Now it's hovering right below the chairman's. You could use this metaphor until every job in America is held by a woman.

The problem with the concept of the glass ceiling is it gives men an excuse for their failure to treat women as equals. What game have you ever played in which your opponent says you're not allowed to win—and you believe him?

It is true that many of us get stopped at a certain point on the way up, but we can't just blame this ceiling. Many complex factors are involved.

Factor one: We have a desire for a life of balance. For example, we're often afraid that if we get to the top, we won't have enough time for the rest of our lives. Another myth. Plenty of middle managers work harder than CEOs. There's no more nor less balance at the pinnacle than halfway up the slope.

Factor two: Because we don't tend to take the positions that lead to the top, because we're less often the rainmakers and more often in those pink-collar jobs, there aren't enough of us sitting in the places that traditionally springboard to CEO. Says Catalyst, the leading not-for-profit organization dealing with women's issues in business, "Only 6.8 percent of all corporate line officers are women . . . if [we had to name] the biggest barrier to women's advancement, that would be it." In other words, more of us have to go after these rainmaking and line positions.

Factor three: a lack of self-confidence. We have to remember that both "I can" and "I can't" are true statements. If you believe you can, you can. If you believe you can't, you can't. By buying into the glass-ceiling concept, or believing that you won't get the promotion, you make an "I can't" statement. Once you move yourself from the world of possibility into the world of impossibility, you make your worst fears come true. You become more cautious, more wary, more alert. Instead of being filled with potential, you're filled with doubt.

Why perpetrate a myth that implies you are the person-who's-done-to instead of the person-who's-doing? Why not just tell your colleagues (male and female alike) there's no such thing as a glass ceiling and that you intend to prove it? Imagine if Columbus had believed the world was flat? Someday they'll say about all the female CEOs of Fortune 500 companies: Imagine if they had bought into that glass-ceiling myth.

Note: Every day it seems I hear about another woman leaving corporate America to go into business for herself. I can certainly understand some of the reasons behind this trend in light of all the difficulties women must face, from the conviction we can't succeed as easily as a man to our need to tend to our families.

But I would ask women to think carefully before they quit. Once you leave the corporate arena, you don't have the same impact on big business, which in turn means you don't have the same impact on the world. If we are going to make our marketing and our products more female and more family-friendly, we need to be part of the team creating them. It's important that we inhabit the places of power in as many positions as possible.

Leaving doesn't help those of us left behind. It doesn't help change the basic way in which big business is done. Large corporations shape our lives. They produce the entertainment shows that we decry, the foods that we deem unhealthy, the advertisements that we find degrading. The more we're around to make key decisions, the more they will go our way.

10|Future (Then and Now)

Some years ago I was in a planning meeting for a not-for-profit organization. We had several important decisions to make about the direction we should take, and I was noticing that a divide had sprung up between the men and women after each issue was discussed.

I had a thought. "When we're talking about 'the future' here," I asked, "what are we talking about?"

The men all said, sometime in the next year. The women all said, many years from now. I was intrigued.

In a meeting at my office the next day, I went around the room asking people to define what the word *future* meant to them. Without exception, the men said six months to a year, the women said ten to fifty years.

Women think of the future in biological human

terms. It's what will happen to us over the years, as well as what will happen to our children and our grandchildren. The dollhouse doesn't end because you stop playing with it. Like the woman in my business course who wanted to extend her game of jacks as long as possible, the most satisfying games are the ones that can be forever prolonged.

Guys' games are time-limited. At some point, when the clock sounds, or when the winner becomes apparent, it's over. End of future. Another future begins with another game.

Women can be great conceptual thinkers. In meetings, we bring up all the possible outcomes, we look at the big picture, we see it all. If no one stops us, we can suggest so many options that a decision becomes impossible. That way we can keep the game going forever.

This approach can irritate the men in the room, who aren't playing our game, and don't want to. If they need a decision now, they may not want to hear what may happen five years hence. They can deal with the complications later. Action has to be taken, now.

There is nothing wrong with thinking of the future as four decades away, unless your boss is thinking four weeks. You don't need to change your conceptual framework. Just stay in the same time zone as the men around you when decisions are being made.

8

HOW TO ENTER AND EXIT THE GAME

*My idea of superwoman is someone
who scrubs her own floors.*
BETTE MIDLER, SINGER AND ACTRESS

SHE CLEANS THE HOUSE, SHE WASHES THE CAR, she reads to her children, she brings the dog to the vet, she takes care of her mother, she cooks the meals, she jogs ten miles a week, she runs a profitable division, she manages her staff, she manages her marriage, she manages the household. She does it all.

No, she doesn't.

We all thought we were supposed to do it all. And some of us can do most of it very well. But I have yet to meet the superwoman who can do everything perfectly. There will always be something missing.

Usually, that something is you. If you're giving your all to everyone in your life, you seldom have the time to care for yourself.

Now that at least one generation of women has learned this lesson, we're beginning to define our limits and boundaries more realistically. There's nothing wrong with choosing to focus on only one part of your life at a time. Maybe you're single, or married and childless, and you want to give your all to your job. Fine. Maybe you've decided to take several years off to have children. Also fine. This is not a cop-out. This is an informed choice.

Many women deride the "mommy track" because it implies that once you slow down to raise a family, you have no chance of getting back on the team. It's either Mommy or vice president, but not both.

But I say it can be both—even if you're off the track for several years. I've known many successful women who put all their energy into their children when they were young, and then reentered the workplace, enhanced and more successful than ever.

In other words, you don't get just one turn on the game board: Your career can be *sequential* as easily as it can be *simultaneous*.

Here is another surprise: You learn an enormous amount while doing all the things connoted by that loaded word, *chores*.

Take my life. When I was young, I had wonderful jobs working for three different congressmen. After that I moved over to the White House's legal counsel's office to draft civil rights legislation. I assumed politics was my life's career.

Then I fell in love with a White House television reporter, and we married. When CBS appointed him their civil-rights correspondent, I, like a good wife, left my career in Washington, D.C., and moved with him to his new job in Atlanta.

Since I'd worked in the White House civil-rights office, I was familiar with the stories my husband was covering. And because I had nothing else to do, I trailed along beside him. CBS had strict antinepotism rules at the time, so there was no chance they could hire me. But one of the ABC reporters, knowing my background, offered me a job at the station. I accepted, and now had a career in television.

Then, two weeks before our first child was due, my husband was appointed CBS's Moscow bureau chief. Once again, my choice was to go wherever my husband went. And once again, CBS wouldn't hire me, but I ended up running the bureau de facto.

Three years later we were back in Atlanta, now with two sons. While I did a little work at ABC, I became pregnant with my third child.

From 1971 to 1978 I took care of our kids, but I also took the occasional odd job, volunteered for a great deal of not-for-profit work, and started a small consulting company out of my kitchen—literally. I came to CNN only when my friends from ABC, who were among CNN's first anchors, asked me to be an editorial producer.

This means I had a period of ten years between full-time jobs. It doesn't mean that my mind went to waste. In fact, I always tell women that everything I ever needed to know about business I learned driving the car pool.

Think about it. Having six kids in one car teaches you how to negotiate: If all of them want a back window seat, you need the brains to work out a solution, unless you don't mind driving to school with a bunch of screaming six-year-olds. This isn't dissimilar from being in the middle of a work crisis while everyone is spinning his or her wheels and has to be quieted down.

You want your yard mowed every week for a low price? That's a wage transaction. You need someone reliable to clean your house? That's a hiring skill. Someone has to take care of your kids? That's learning how to delegate. Buying the groceries on a budget teaches fiscal responsibility. Dealing with an insurance company after an accident prepares you for financial negotiations. Knowing how and when to send thank-you notes teaches you the importance of making your staff feel appreciated. And pulling off a dinner party for twelve on four hours notice takes as much coordination as anything I've ever done at CNN.

Not only are these tasks similar to those you do at the office, they're often performed under greater pressure because of the assumption that household chores require no real skills—society has diminished these jobs so thoroughly that we seldom acknowledge the tangible talents they demand.

(According to a recent study by Edelman Financial Services, as cook, financial manager, psychologist, and bus driver, American mothers should pull in $508,700 per year, based on average U.S. salaries.)

You don't have to live your life as though you only have one chance. Do as much as you can, or want—and in your own time frame. But remember: If you try to do it all, it won't all be perfect.

Recently I gave a speech to a group of women I had addressed five years earlier. After it was over, one of the women, Jennifer, reminded me that she had asked for some personal advice the last time we had met: Her career had been going very well, but she'd just given birth to her second child and wanted to work part-time so she could stay at home.

The problem was that Jennifer had a competitor—

a childless woman who Jennifer was convinced would take her job if she stepped off the track. She reminded me that I had told her you can always get a new job, but that you can't get new children.

I also advised Jennifer not to have regrets. She was making her own decision, and it was one she could be proud of. No one was forcing her to leave.

Now Jennifer told me that she had been working part-time for six years and was about to return full-time. The irony of the situation was that her new job was to replace the other woman, who had indeed been promoted, just as Jennifer had feared. But that woman was expecting a baby herself, and was taking a few years off to stay home.

I don't mean to suggest that every story has a happy ending. Of course it doesn't. My point is that there was a time when *none* of these tales of the business world ended well for women. This is a healthy indicator of change.

A sequential career means that when you're ready, you can return to work you love able to see new possibilities, open to new ideas. It had never entered my mind to enter television. But when I did, I saw that my experience in politics had prepared me well for my new job—it taught me to think like a politician. When I dealt with Capitol Hill, I was able to understand how the subtleties worked without having to ask.

A lot of young women feel that if they leave a full-time job, their former equals will end up far ahead of them when they return. This harkens back to the ten-year-plan issue (see Chapter 3: Set the Right Goal). If you think everything is part of a long-term strategy, and each move is an incremental step up the ladder, you miss the fact that almost anything in life can be a learning experience. A side road only becomes a dead end when you forget that side roads often lead to exciting new places.

There are times, however, when you want to leave your job, not because it's time to raise a family, or because you've fallen in love with someone who lives across the country, or because you must take care of your aging parents. Sometimes, you just want out. Other times, the powers-that-be make it clear they want you out. A recent study shows that the average American will hold eight different jobs over his or her lifetime.

The signs are everywhere: The good assignments no longer come your way; you're left out of important meetings; the boss stops asking for your opinion; the smart women in the company no longer see you as their mentor but have found someone younger.

Or there are internal signs: You resent your boss, you can't stand your hours. Soon you're playing the same recording over and over in your head—the one that goes, "I hate what I do. I hate my job. I hate my career."

If these are your thoughts as you wake up in the morning, you need to take action.

Guys plan for these moments. In fact, just as they develop a strategy to make the team, they develop one to leave. They've played enough games to know that you have to be ready to make a proactive move whenever necessary. In the world of television, whenever a network is in trouble, it always seems to be the men who are quick to get out the resumes, to make the new contacts, to call up the headhunters. They're ready to sell themselves at a moment's notice.

Think of it this way: Men and women approach jobs the way they approach their relationships; men, who are polygamy-oriented, always look for multiple opportunities; women, who are monogamy-oriented, want their job to be long-lasting. We can become so attached to our company that sometimes we refuse to leave even when we're miserable. This may make us seem like wonderfully loyal employees, but it can also turn us into victims. We want to stay and prove ourselves, but in the meantime they push us too hard and pay us too little. We're miserable, we're indignant. But we often don't go anywhere.

Why? Probably because we find risk so frightening.

But leaving is often the only right thing.

And it often pays off. My friend Jo in telecommunications hated her job for years. Her particular tape—"I do all the work and my boss gets all the glory"—ran through her head every morning on the way to work and every evening on the way back. She was well paid, but mistreated, and embittered.

Jo braced herself, entered her boss's office, and told him she had found another job. She then joined a start-up company where she was extremely happy—for a year. The company went belly up, and she was jobless, back at square zero.

Or was she? Here was her (and our) worst fantasy come true; no different from the received wisdom that says if you leave your husband or partner you'll be alone in the world.

But the reality was, Jo had a new job in a month—and her new employer hired her exactly because of her entrepreneurial nature. After all, she'd left a major company to work with a start-up. And, she brought with her everything she'd learned in that tough start-up year.

She took a risk. The worst happened. She still won.

Leave when you know you must. But leave intelligently. Too often, when we do reach the breaking point, we take action impulsively. "I'll get back at them," we think. "I'll cook their goose. I'll just walk out right now and that will show them."

You can't storm off the field. A little boy who walks out on the team is so scorned by the other players that he learns his lesson: If you're on the team, you stay there until it makes sense to go. When you leave your company in the lurch, your associates will consider you disloyal, untrustworthy, a quitter. That is not a reputation to cultivate.

Instead, come up with a sensible plan. Call up your contacts. Take tests. Send out your resume. See a headhunter. Read the employment section of the newspaper—but not wishfully. Read it purposefully. If you see something interesting, respond. When you line up the new position, tell your boss considerately and intelligently. Let him know how much you have learned from working with him— but that now, it's time for both of you to move on. If you were careful about picking the right boss (remember—a good boss is more important than a good job), he should understand the fait accompli without making you feel guilty.

Be advised that if you're unhappy, it's unlikely that your job performance is solid. Tell yourself you're doing the company a favor by gracefully orchestrating your exit and by giving your boss the chance to bring in someone who can do your job with fresh enthusiasm.

A good boss wants to know if you're miserable. Personally, I have a rule for all my staff: If I'm not the first one to know when people are unhappy, they're in trouble.

As risky and unpleasant as it may seem, if you plan your escape well, you may be making the least risky move of your career. Both you and your company will prosper from it.

GAME HINT: One way to leave well is to stop thinking of your current job as The Big Career—that can make you feel even more frustrated as your discontent grows. Tell yourself it is simply the means to an end. In other words, it is just The Paycheck.

Think: This isn't the right place for me, but I need to pay the rent (or save for graduate school or create a retirement fund) so I can't just walk out.

When you regard the job as a financial boon rather than a lifetime commitment, it becomes much less loaded with meaning. That makes it easier to come to work and eventually, to go.

Nineteen ninety-nine was a big year in professional sports. Or at least it was a big year for athletes to leave them. Michael Jordan, Wayne Gretzky, Cal Ripken, Jr., and John Elway all retired from their professions of basketball, ice hockey, baseball, and football respectively. Two of them may have been the best ever to play their games, but that's an argument for another book.

Apart from greatness, what all of these men definitely have in common was that they were not forced to retire. While none of them was at the top of his game, each could still play better than most of his peers, pull down a huge salary, and make his fans deliriously happy. Each also understood it was time to make an exit.

There is seldom a good reason to linger once you can no longer play your best game. That's true for football and hockey, and it's true for business.

Our careers progress in stages: first comes the heady entry-level job, when you're like a child in a candy shop and everything is exciting. Following that comes workplace adolescence, when you're on your way up, but you don't know how far you'll go. Eventually, as you reach adulthood, you're at the top of your game.

Then one day you notice that it's becoming more of an effort to come to the office, that you don't push to be included in exciting new projects, that you're not interested in proving yourself, that your attention is increasingly focused on interests outside the workplace. You're no longer a young lion going in for the kill. The only thing you're killing is time.

How many of us have the self-awareness to know the game is coming to an end? And how many of us are fully prepared to make that break when it appears inevitable? You know that Michael

Jordan has spent the last decade making sure his financial house is in order (admittedly an easier thing to do when you make 50 million dollars a year). Is yours?

For most women, the answer is no. Planning our financial futures has meant having our husbands or partners take care of it, just as our fathers handled the money for our mothers. Even most of us who aren't in a relationship are still hoping that some White Knight will come charging along and save us from thinking about insurance, investments, retirement, and estate taxes.

Please! White Knights went out with girdles and bouffant hairdos. Unless you're very lucky, you alone are responsible for your financially secure old age. Even if you have a partner or husband, you can't be certain that he will be around to take care of you when your career is over. Why take the chance?

From the very beginning of the game, start planning to end it. You make sure your home is in order. Get your financial house together, too. The process takes many years, and the variables are constantly changing.

Maybe today you think you'll retire at 60, maybe tomorrow you'll make that 70, or 55, or 80. You can make continual adjustments, but you have to be absolutely sure you can afford to retire when the time comes to do it.

Buy one of the many books about financial planning. Talk to savvy friends and colleagues. Start collecting names of skilled advisors. The monetary aspect of the retirement game is something no women can afford to neglect.

If most of us have a difficult time dealing with the financial issues connected to our postcareer lives, we find it even more daunting to confront the issue of status. In other words, your job is not who you are. Your job is what you do.

Sound simple? It's not. Men have been in business for years, and few of them have learned this. I've seen hundreds of men face retirement, and even the smartest among them, my own father included, never truly mastered it.

Over the years I've learned that, to most of the world, I am not Gail Evans, but Gail-Evans-Executive-Vice-President-of-CNN. I don't exist without the rest of those words that follow my given name.

Sometimes I fall for this error myself. I've come to depend on that hyphenated phrase to land hard-to-get dinner reservations, to make a big impression at social events, to cultivate contacts and sources. It's an identification that works, it gets me into tough places, it makes people pay attention to me. I can't pretend I don't like it.

But do I truly know that those strung-together words are not who I am? I won't know that fully until I leave my job, and become just plain Gail Evans.

Resolving this issue should be a woman's gift to the workplace. We like to say that our identity as a woman is defined by all of our various relationships: as a mother with our children, as a friend with our community, as a lover with our partner. I have noticed, however, that as women have become more powerful, we've begun to emulate men when it comes to wrapping our identity around our job, giving up other means of valuing ourselves that have historically provided us with perspective.

But as we rise in the business world, along with the possibility that we will handle retirement the old-fashioned way, comes another prospect: that we will rewrite the rules of business, and particularly the rules for retirement. As long as we keep in mind our gift for valuing the totality of our lives, as long as we don't believe that we are only as good as our jobs, we can turn retirement, even retirement from highly successful careers, into a great adventure. Instead of feeling bereft, we can make it a time to investigate other parts of our personalities: Maybe we will go back to work part-time and mentor young women. Maybe we will return to our families. Maybe we will discover hidden talents and start new careers.

Let's take advantage of our discovery that

careers can be sequential, and not only simultaneous, and make this sequence of our life the best it
can be. Why shouldn't we use all our gifts as
women to make retirement every bit as productive
and empowering as our work years?

9

THE FINAL TWO RULES

*Because of their age-long training in human relations—
for that is what feminine intuition really is—women have
a special contribution to make to any group enterprise.*

MARGARET MEAD, ANTHROPOLOGIST

1 | Be a Woman

The other day I had lunch with one of the members of the Atlanta Braves (the team is owned by our company). We had a wonderful discussion covering a wide range of subjects—his family life, his background, his dreams, as well as mine.

A few nights later I attended a game with one of the CNN sports anchors. When the player ran out on the field, I said, "There's my new buddy!" and told the anchor about our lunch.

The sportscaster was startled. "Are you kidding?" he said. "We never talk about stuff like that." He then debriefed me on how the guys talk to each other and the press. It was all pure guy-to-guy conversation: just the facts, just the stats; no emotion, no connection.

Later I realized that my talk with the Brave had been so thoughtful because I had allowed myself to be a woman. I didn't pretend I was some kind of sports genius and I didn't try to talk like a man. I asked him how his family was dealing with his recent trade to Atlanta, how his wife was coping with the move, how his kids were adjusting to school. I tried to create a relationship with him.

So often I am struck by the personal nature of the discussions women can have with men while doing business, and I'm confident that these conversations enhance our working relationships. This doesn't mean the men leave thinking we're not savvy or astute. But it can leave them feeling safer around us. They understand that besides being business associates, we're also real women who can take a genuine interest in their wives, their families, and the problems that they don't discuss with other men.

All the smart women I know in business agree: By allowing the natural, nurturing part of yourself to be available, you can build genuine relationships with the men you work with and for. This means that they will trust you and your opinions, which in turn can give you greater access to them.

I intensify that relationship by acting true to my instincts as a mother. Since I love kids, I always keep children's books on my shelves, which means that employees working on weekends or holidays often bring their kids to my office. This part of my personality helps soothe hurt feelings when I'm yelling at those children's parents a few days later. Like every boss, I have irrational moments. But how angry can you truly become when you can also picture your red-faced, screaming boss holding your daughter on her lap?

Use every one of your natural traits. Use your win/win attitude about life to make everyone you work with feel like a valued member of the team. Use your social skills. The receptionist has a new hairstyle or the cleaning woman is back after having a baby—acknowledge these events. People remember, and reward, kindness, when it's genuine.

Most of all, use your intuition. Men don't learn about intuition—after all, there's no such phrase as "men's intuition." Women do; we're fundamentally more intuitive than men. I doubt this is an innate attribute, however. Most likely it derives from our orientation toward relationships, and the attention we pay to people's bodies, voices, minds. When the baby is crying at night, we need to know whether that cry indicates serious distress or basic fussing. When our ten-year-old says he hates school, we have to know whether he's having a bad day or he's having a bad life. If our teenager has had three minor fender benders in the last two months, we know he'll probably do it again. Saying, "Be careful," before he takes a step doesn't mean you're a genius. It means you've been carefully watching and have noticed patterns.

Intuition is the ability to be aware of what's happening around you at the moment. It means listening for the tiniest nuances of a particular situation, knowing how to read body and mind signals, and your own signals, too.

Surprising as it may seem, there aren't a lot of great mysteries in business. It's not difficult to get inside most people's heads. If you're truly listening and looking, most people are more revealing than they realize. Through body language, voice tone, words, and subtext, they'll tell you everything you need to know.

Intuition is one of the most powerful tools women have in the marketplace. To use it, all you have to do is listen—not just with your ears, but with your gut.

So employ your female instincts to your advantage—as long as you understand the effect these will have on the men in your office. It's one thing to be privately nurturing with a male peer whose work is faltering, but don't do it in a public forum or you'll embarrass both of you.

Business relationships are first and foremost office alliances. This doesn't mean that they're not genuine, only that they exist to help all of you build a better, more profitable, more enjoyable workplace.

2 | Be Yourself

Whenever male writers want to create a female character of interest, they make her the most powerful, the most beautiful, or the most treacherous. She becomes a Lady Macbeth, a Helen of Troy, a Becky Sharp.

Female writers, however, paint such a heroine with integrity. Think of Jane Austen's Elizabeth Bennet, Virginia Woolf's Mrs. Ramsay, or Edith Wharton's Lily Bart: women whom other women admire because of their strong, ethical character.

I certainly wouldn't say that women have more integrity than men. That's a person-by-person judgment. But perhaps, from a sociobiological perspective, integrity is important to us because the man who has most integrity is most likely to be the one whose promises of fidelity are authentic, and therefore the best mate. Perhaps we care for integrity because we grow up believing that it is the foundation of any relationship, and relationships form the cornerstone of our existence. Or, perhaps the concept of valorizing integrity is truly hardwired into our genetic makeup.

One of the several dictionary definitions of integrity is: the quality or condition of being whole and undivided, completeness; the state of being unimpaired, soundness.

To me, this means being true to yourself, and being your true self everywhere you go, including the office.

The woman who tries to change her inner self to fit into her work environment will always be the proverbial square peg. There she is, pretending to be a tigress, but in reality she's a pussycat wanting to be loved. She's a walking hypocrite, and she knows it. The lie makes her miserable, others pick up on that, and soon no one—neither her office mates nor the woman—know who she really is.

No amount of hiding or pretending will change a person's inner self. A woman who constantly re-creates herself, who tries to be something other than who she is, will never be comfortable inside her own skin—or anywhere else.

Let's say a woman who's about to go out on a date with a new boyfriend spends hours beforehand trying to figure out how she should present herself. Flirt? Intellectual? Career woman?

Homebody? By the time that evening is over, no matter what role she has assumed, it's unlikely that she or her date enjoyed themselves.

The same principle applies in the business world. If you funnel all your energy into propping up some counterfeit image, you'll have little left over for your job.

Still, many women create an alter ego because the "real me," they tell me, couldn't be successful. I say the "fake you" won't be successful either. Do you think you'll prosper every day you bring in some fantasy identity? Perhaps that's why we read so many stories about female executives who drop out of corporate life because they don't feel fulfilled. Perhaps many of these women never revealed their true selves at work. How good could it feel to think you're an impersonator all day?

There is always a temptation to hide from ourselves, to have self-doubts, to tell ourselves, "I don't really know who I am, so I'll just be whatever seems most promotable."

But others can spot the ruse. We all have instincts that tell us who is genuine and who isn't, just as we sense this about ourselves. Sometimes, when I've said something clearly insincere, I catch myself and think, "I can't believe I just said that."

I remember the very first time I allowed myself to be completely, unadulteratedly me. It happened while a dozen male executives and I were watching a tape of a new CNN program designed to appeal to women. The show featured a well-known model and chronicled her day as an average woman, dropping off her child at day care, taking care of her chores, buying groceries, and so on.

After the tape aired, all the men in the room expressed their admiration for the show. Then they turned to me.

"What do you think?" they asked. Translation: "What does The Woman think?"

"I hate it," I said.

They assumed I was kidding. "Come on, what do you really think?" they insisted.

I reiterated my reaction. "Women aren't going to buy this," I said.

"What should we change?" they asked.

"I hate the whole thing," I said. "It isn't a matter of changing anything. It just doesn't work."

Normally I would have made suggestions on how to improve each segment, how to change the interstitial portion, and analyzed the impact of the show from a business perspective. But this was one time I didn't feel like speaking male-talk. I knew the show wasn't going to work, because it wasn't credible. No woman in her right mind was going to believe that this stunning, privileged woman shared any of the daily problems the audi-

ence faced—much less even bought a bag of groceries.

So for the first time in my career I gave myself
permission to be myself, to say what I truly believed,
and deal with the consequences.

What I learned was that no one disliked me for
it, or stopped asking for my opinion, or fired me. I
didn't have to keep making myself up. I had
enough credibility that I could express myself honestly, in my language.

Being yourself doesn't mean that you can't and
won't succeed in a male world. It does mean you
have to find a comfortable fit between who you are
and the environment in which you work.

Nor does it mean you have to obey every one of
the suggestions in this book. You don't have to toot
your own horn, you don't have to speak up, you
don't have to be a team player. It's fine to work
anonymously in a corner or a back room, as long as
you fully grasp the consequences of your actions.
If you love your quiet job because you can come
and go as you please, get your four percent raise
every year, and have plenty of time for your life,
that's fine. But if your ambition is to become CFO,
CEO, or chairman of the board, you've got to make
noise.

This book is about learning to make noise, and
also, learning to make choices. Think of my advice

as clothes you are trying on. Does the rule fit? Do you look good in it? Is it you?

Last spring at Neiman Marcus I saw an array of jackets and matching skirts in lovely, vibrant colors, all cheerfully lined up right next to a rack of the neutral-toned pants suits I normally wear. My immediate urge was to buy something in one of those wonderful colors, but then I thought of all those hot Atlanta afternoons and how I'd have to wear panty hose if I wore a skirt.

Even though I wanted to think of myself as a person who would wear bright colors, as I looked at the mirror, I knew that's not who I am. I'm the gray pants suit woman—at least at this point in my life.

My daughter tries on dozens of almost identical white blouses and then finds the one she feels is her. No one else can see a difference. When you try on these directions, do the same. If you don't like the way you look, know that many other women don't either. But also know that if you reject the outfit altogether, you may regret it 15 years down the road.

Even if you feel stuck at a company where you don't always feel comfortable, you can still try to find a place while remaining true to yourself.

Why do so many of us go into public relations, or human resources, or creative services? Some feminists say it's because men shuttle us off to the pink-collar ghetto, end of story. But I think that being in an area such as human resources lets us appreciate our impact on others. Today, for example, you may have helped a single mother find day care so she could keep her job, or you led an unhappy junior executive to a satisfying position in a new department, and you feel terrific about it.

As you scrutinize the job market, do the same for yourself. Say you were a passionate environmentalist in college, and now you take a job at a company considered a major polluter. Will you be happy? Or do you really just want to make money? Admit it to yourself. There's nothing inherently wrong with that choice.

The other day I interviewed a young woman who told me that she was looking for a job where she could make as much money and meet as many eligible guys as possible. She hoped to marry within a few years, but in the meantime, she wanted to live well. I don't care what the job is, she said, as long as it fills those requirements.

A colleague of mine thought this job-seeker was shameless, but I was impressed—this woman knew herself. A lot of us can recognize ourselves in her remarks, but we may be afraid to admit it, because her ambitions are so bold and sound so inappropriate.

"I want to work in a socially responsible company," we say, and we mean it. But maybe not forever. This young woman used to care about saving the world too in her twenties. Now she wants to save herself. And maybe she'll change again.

If you don't want to be a martyr at the office, decide what matters to you. Talk aloud to yourself. Speaking your vision gets you halfway there. What do you dream about? Write down your fantasies. Make lists. We've been trained to be in touch with everyone else's needs rather than our own. But if you don't know what you want from the business world, you'll never get it. Believe me, no one else will get it for you.

The ultimate satisfaction for a businesswoman is to feel good about herself, her bosses, and the company she works for. It's difficult to find this match in the large corporation. Stack the odds in your favor by living into your fullest sense of yourself. See everything as possible. Be the person who says she can get it done. Don't be caught in the old myth about what you can't do. Create your own myths about what you can do. If you're blocked, sit back and figure out how to make a creative detour. Never accept a stop sign as a brick wall. Accept that sometimes you have to back up to go forward. Know there's nothing that you can't do if you set your mind to it.

Women have so much to offer the world. Someday, when phrases such as glass ceiling no longer exist, we will change the workplace in unimaginable ways. In the meantime, remember: Have a good time. Be yourself. Love your life. And love the game.

ACKNOWLEDGMENTS

So many people have helped me throughout my career and throughout the course of this book. I thank each and every one of you, and wish I could cite every name. There are a few people, however, I must single out:

Jeanne Mintz, my first boss, who taught me that a woman could be anything she wanted; former congressman William Fitts Ryan, who showed me that you never have to give up your values and your ideals, no matter how great the pressure; Don Farmer and Chris Curle, for their friendship and everything they taught me about television, and also for giving me (more than once) the opportunity to make television news a career; Burt Reinhardt, for his wisdom, his smile, and his unfailing, quiet support; Ed Turner, a brilliant writer and editorial maestro; Tom Johnson, a man of true integrity who believed in me and gave me a place at the table; Rick Kaplan, a great egalitarian and superb television producer; Ted Turner and Gerry Levin, whom I feel privileged to work for every day; Wendy Guarisco, a truly fine researcher; the Landmark Forum, where I learned that personal and professional breakthroughs are always attainable; Jan Miller, a terrific agent and wonderful friend; Suzanne Oaks and Bob Asahina, my excellent editors at Broadway Books; Jane Leavey, Bobbie Goldin, and Jackie Damgaard, for their support and friendship; Jarvin Levison, for his understanding and his legal guidance; my father, whose pride in his daughter still makes me smile today; my daughters-in-law Laurie and Kathy, and their beautiful children Drew, Alec, and Sarah, who bring joy to my life every day; my sister Bonnie Reeves and my sister-in-law Judith Evans, both successful executives who provided me with a glimpse into other parts of corporate America; Bob Evans, for his support and encouragement; John Reeves, Eli Evans, and Josh Evans, the wonderful men in my family; my mother-in-law Sara Evans, the consummate businesswoman; Alvin Goldstein, my guru, my coach, my best friend, and the person who opened me to the world of possibility; and Goode, who never tires of hearing my stories.

I also want to mention some of my many CNN friends and co-workers, past and present, including: Wendy Whitworth, Judy Milestone, Diane Durham, Lucy Spiegel, Jennifer Zeidman, Jennifer Maguire, Teya Ryan, Sue Bunda, Pat Mitchell, Sue Binford, Catherine Crier, Greta Van Susteren, Julia Sprunt, Judy Woodruff, Eason

Jordan, Don Smith, Steve Korn, Rick Davis, Frank Sesno, Bob Furnad, Robin Tanner, Alma Scroggins, Jane Maxwell, Dave Kohler, Patrick Reap, Carol Buckland, Chris Mould, Sid Bedingfield, Keith McAllister, Jill Neff, Joy di Benedetto, Gail Chalef, Cory Charles, Susan Toffler, Bonnie Anderson, David Bernknopf, Samantha Robinson, Renee Davis, Jodi Fleisig, Ashley Van Buren, Betsy Goldman, Joan Klunder, Cindy Patrick, Susan Grant, and Lauren Oltarsh.

And finally: Gene Stone, who bravely took me by the hand and made it possible for me to write this book. I am in awe of his ability to turn my conversations into the written word. Most important, working with him was great fun. He never failed to offer the right degree of support and friendship.

ABOUT THE AUTHOR

As executive vice president of the CNN Newsgroup, Gail Evans oversees the domestic networks' program and talent development. Additionally she is responsible for CNN's talk show programs and the booking and research departments. Evans's programs have received numerous awards, including a Commendation Award from American Women in Radio and Television and the Breakthrough Award for Women, Men, and Media, as well as several Emmy nominations. She lives in Atlanta.